Illustrating Paul's Letter to the Romans

James E. Hightower, Jr.
Compiler

BROADMAN PRESS
Nashville, Tennessee

4222-51

ISBN: 0-8054-2251-X
Dewey Decimal Classification: 227.1
Subject Headings: BIBLE. N.T. ROMANS
Library of Congress Catalog Card Number: 84-7074

Printed in the United States of America

Library of Congress Cataloging in Publication Data
Main entry under title:

Illustrating Paul's letter to the Romans.

Includes index.
1. Bible. N.T. Romans—Homiletical use.
2. Homiletical illustrations. I. Hightower, James E.
BS2665.4.I44 1984 251′.08 84-7074
ISBN 0-8054-2251-X (pbk.)

Contributors

Raymond H. Bailey, associate professor of communication, The Southern Baptist Theological Seminary, Louisville, Kentucky

Robert W. Bailey, pastor, Southside Baptist Church, Birmingham, Alabama

Bill Bruster, pastor, Central Baptist Church of Bearden, Knoxville, Tennessee

Harold T. Bryson, professor of preaching, New Orleans Baptist Theological Seminary, New Orleans, Louisiana

James E. Carter, pastor, University Baptist Church, Fort Worth, Texas

Hardy Denham, president, Pulpit Ministries, Inc., Newton, Mississippi

J. Dixon Free, pastor, First Baptist Church, Ormond Beach, Florida

J. B. Fowler, editor, *The New Mexican Baptist,* Albuquerque, New Mexico

Elmer L. Gray, editor, *The California Southern Baptist,* Fresno, California

Jack Gulledge, editor, *Mature Living,* Nashville, Tennessee

Brian L. Harbour, pastor, First Baptist Church, Pensacola, Florida

Roger Lovette, pastor, First Baptist Church, Clemson, South Carolina

David Matthews, pastor, First Baptist Church, Greenville, South Carolina

Alton H. McEachern, pastor, First Baptist Church, Greensboro, North Carolina

Gage McMahon, free-lance writer, New Orleans, Louisiana

W. Wayne Price, pastor, Williamsburg Baptist Church, Williamsburg, Virginia

Ernest D. Standerfer, director of stewardship development promotion, Stewardship Commission, SBC, Nashville, Tennessee

William P. Tuck, pastor, Saint Matthews Baptist Church, Louisville, Kentucky

Bill D. Whittaker, pastor, International Baptist Church, Manila, Philippines

James A. Young, chairman, Department of Religion, Louisiana college, Pineville, Louisiana

Introduction

Why This Book?

This book is a sequel to *Illustrating the Gospel of Matthew*. Its purpose is to help pastors shed light on Romans, a pivotal book of the New Testament.

This book of sermon illustrations is certainly not exhaustive. No pastor should become dependent on other people's illustrations; the best illustrations come from you and your personal experiences. In that spirit, this book is offered as a tool in ministry. Hopefully, it will be one resource you can readily use while constructing a sermon on Romans.

Who Are the Writers?

An effort was made to include persons from many areas of Southern Baptist leadership to write this volume. Pastors, missionaries, denominational writers, free-lance writers, state paper editors, and professors in our colleges and seminaries are represented here. Hopefully, their experience in ministry will give fresh, lively insight to the Book of Romans.

The persons who helped write this book are given a particular thanks. Without their efforts this project would not have lived.

How to Use This Book

This book of illustrations has several unique features to maximize its effectiveness. First, the illustrations are all related to one book of the Bible,

Romans. Second, the illustrations are listed in chronological order from Romans 1:1 to Romans 16:27. Third, each illustration is classified by subject. An example of this is Romans 1:16—Power. Finally, a subject index is included. This allows the pastor to use this book even when preaching outside of the Book of Romans. It is my hope that these features will help pastors in telling the good news of Jesus Christ.

An Arab proverb says, "He is the best speaker who can turn the ear into an eye." *Illustrating Paul's Letter to the Romans* will help you turn ears into eyes.

JAMES HIGHTOWER
Compiler

Romans 1:8-12 Support

In many communities, people band together to form support groups. These range in diversity from neighborhood watch programs endeavoring to prevent crime to groups addressing such problems as alcoholism, weight control, or delinquency. Churches frequently offer classes in spiritual growth or in similar topics designed to aid members' development.

The concept of these church support groups points to the relationship between Paul and the church at Rome. In their faith, they found mutual strength and encouragement to face the difficulties of their lives.

GAGE MCMAHON

Romans 1:8-15 Indebted

Years ago a wealthy student attending Williams College was accused of defacing some of the college property. When he went in to see the college president, Mark Hopkins, he arrogantly whipped out his checkbook and asked how much was it going to cost him to pay for the damages.

President Hopkins ordered the young man to sit down and exclaimed: "No man can pay for what he receives here. Can you pay for the sacrifices of Colonel Williams who founded the college? Can you pay for the half-paid professors who have remained here to teach when they could have gone elsewhere? Every student here is a charity case!"

How often all of us forget that. We are indebted to so many, including parents, teachers, neighbors, farmers, builders, doctors, and countless others, and especially to God for his loving grace.

WILLIAM P. TUCK

Romans 1:16 Good News

The word *gospel* flows like a mighty stream through all the letters that Paul wrote. That word, we know, means good news. Because it was such good news, Paul could not keep silent but wrote and preached and lived that great message until his dying breath.

Halford Luccock captures something of that spirit when he told that he had carried in his mind for thirty years a picture of something that happened once in a New Haven hospital. He said that a man came running down the hall of the corridor with a chart he had taken from the foot of a patient's bed. He grabbed Luccock by the arm and showed him the chart and said, "Look! Her temperature's going down! Her temperature's going down!" Luccock said he did not know who he meant by "her," but she must be someone the man loved. He said he had never seen the man before and never saw him after that time. But, the preacher said, to his dying day he would never forget the spectacle of a man so overwhelmed with good news that he had to grab the first stranger and tell him all about it.

ROGER LOVETTE

Romans 1:16 Power

George PoBa, from Burma, recalls a story told by his grandmother. At the height of World War II, a Christian family who lived in a jungle village was getting ready to celebrate Christmas. One night they were startled by the excited barking of the dogs and, above the noise, a human cry for help.

In the darkness, they found a badly wounded soldier. They took him in and gave him their best care.

The next morning they discovered, to their horror, that the wounded man was a notoriously cruel Japanese commandant of a prisoner-of-war camp in the area. His camp had been overrun by the Burmese guerrilla forces, and he had been nearly killed in the attack.

Not knowing this, the Burmese guerrillas arrived in the village, and this family had to help host them. Meanwhile, the Japanese commandant, constantly fearful for his life, was kept in hiding.

After three days the guerrillas left, rested and with rations replenished. Puzzled by the protective action of this family, the Japanese commandant asked for an explanation. The head of the family told the unlikely guest that they were Christians and were taught by their Master to love everyone, even their enemies. Besides, they were preparing to celebrate his birth, so it was especially important to share his love.

The commandant remained with the family until he was well and strong enough to leave. Also, during that time, the power of the gospel provided another kind of healing, and he left with a new allegiance. Like the Wise Men of old, he went back to his own country a different way.

David Matthews

Romans 1:16 Change

C. T. Studd was an English socialite who went to hear Dwight L. Moody preach because he lost a bet with a friend. As he sat under the preaching of this colorful American evangelist, God touched Studd's heart. As he left that night Studd said to his friend, "The fellow has just told me everything I've ever done! I'll come and hear him again." He did so night after night until he was converted.

Studd lived just two years after that, but it was said at his funeral that he did more in two years than most Christians do in a lifetime. He withdrew from the social club he had been attending. He turned the great hall at Tedworth into a meeting room for Christian discussion. He wrote his friends about their spiritual condition. He laughed when they responded rudely. He called on his tailor and shirtmaker and the man from whom he had bought his cigars and spoke of Christ. His coachman gave this assessment of his life. "All I can say is that though there's the same skin, there's a new man inside."

That is a living example of the declaration of Paul in the Book of Romans: "For I am not ashamed of the gospel: it is the power of God for salvation to every one who has faith" (RSV).

BRIAN L. HARBOUR

Romans 1:16 Unashamed of Christ

In a day like ours, when it is often easy and safe to be identified with Christ, it is difficult to imagine how hard it was for the early Christians to bear witness for Christ. An ancient painting drawn on a stone wall was unearthed a number of years ago. The painting revealed how unpopular it was to be a Christian in the first century. This particular painting had a picture of Jesus hanging on a cross, and in place of the head of Christ was a picture of a donkey. Underneath were written these words: "Alex the Jew worships his god." With this kind of disdain and ridicule directed against the early Christians, many of them were often ashamed of being Christians. Paul challenged them to hold up their heads and declare: "I am proud of the gospel" (Moffatt).

WILLIAM P. TUCK

Romans 1:16-17 Revolution

Paul's Letter to the Romans has been a useful means of bringing many people to faith in Christ. Also, the Book of Romans has been the catalyst to bring Christian renewal and reformation. The letter contains the basic truths which Paul proclaimed, taught, and wrote throughout the ancient world. God used Romans to help a first-century pagan world.

Paul's Letter to the Romans made a profound impact on a man by the name of Augustine. A small child gave Augustine a book which contained Romans 13:13-14. It spoke to his heart. Augustine reported that Romans was a influential instrument in his conversion experience. Augustine became bishop of Hippo and a significant preacher of the fourth century. Romans played an important role in the development of Augustine's thought.

Martin Luther, a sixteenth-century churchman, was disturbed over how to have a right relationship with God. Upon careful study of Romans and especially Romans 1:17, Luther understood the great truth of justification by faith. Luther's study of Romans radically transformed the troubled monk and influenced him to become a militant reformer of the church.

An eighteenth-century Anglican priest struggled with doubt. For over ten years Wesley sought inner peace. One evening in 1738, John Wesley attended a Moravian Bible study in Aldergate Street in London. While some layman read from Martin Luther's preface to the Romans, Wesley said he was changed within his heart. Again the Letter of Romans was the instrument for initiating an Evangelical awakening that transformed religious life in England and around the world.

In the early part of the twentieth century, a Swiss pastor named Karl Barth discovered a new world within the Bible. Barth concentrated upon the Roman letter, producing his momentous *Rommerbrief* (commentary on Romans) in 1919. The commentary emphasized the significance of Romans, applying its message to contemporary problems.

Paul's Letter to the Romans has been used by God to bring revolution. It affected the first-century world, provided the basic theology for fourth-century theology, used as proof for justification by faith in the sixteenth century, and helped bring people to the Bible in solving human problems during the twentieth century.

HAROLD BRYSON

Romans 1:16-17 Power

How would you like to read your own obituary? One morning in 1888, Alfred B. Nobel, the Swedish chemist who invented dynamite, the man who grew wealthy by producing weapons of destruction, awoke to read his own obituary! It seems that his brother had died, and a French reporter carelessly reported the death of the wrong brother!

Anyone would have been shaken. But to Alfred B. Nobel, the shock was overwhelming. He suddenly saw himself as others saw him—an amazing discovery that few persons make. He was to the world "the dynamite king," the industrialist who became rich from explosives. So far as the general public was concerned, this was "the whole story" of Nobel's life. To the world he was quite simply a "merchant of death."

Horrified by his obituary, Nobel resolved to do something different with his life. His last will and testament expressed his life's ideals. Five Nobel Prizes are awarded each year, the most notable of which is the peace prize.[1]

Nobel named his invention *dynamite*—taken from the Greek word that means power. That is the very word that Paul used to describe the gospel in Romans 1:16.

James E. Carter

Romans 1:16-17 Not Ashamed of the Gospel

One way to emphasize something is to say that the opposite of it is not true. That is a grammatical device called litotes. Paul used that device to tell how great his confidence was in the gospel of Jesus Christ.

Here's the way that works: to say something is absolutely clean, you say it's spotless. If a diamond is perfect, you say it is without flaw. Jesus emphasized the honesty and trustworthiness of Nathanael by saying he was an Israelite without guile.

How much did Paul value the gospel? How certain was he about its power to save everyone who would believe? How much did he himself believe that the gospel is the revelation of God's righteousness?

Paul's confidence in the gospel of Jesus Christ was so great he said that nothing about it caused him the least embarrassment. He was convinced it would prove to be completely satisfactory to anyone who accepted it.

Elmer L. Gray

Romans 1:16-17; 5:1-2 Faith

It has been said that Paul, Augustine, and Martin Luther were the greatest theologians in the history of the church. Each felt deeply the devastating effects of sin and, therefore, were able to glory in the grace of the Lord Jesus Christ.

Luther was plagued by an overwhelming sense of guilt. He saw God as an angry judge who had passed a sentence of death for sin. Luther sought freedom from his sin in the sacraments. He experienced all the sacraments which his church could offer him. He became a monk in the hope that he could earn the salvation he so desperately needed. But his knowledge of God's perfection and his own unworthiness only intensified his fear of death and damnation. As a monk he fasted, spent long hours in prayer, inflicted physical deprivation and punishment on his body. He went to confession so often that the other monks would hide when they saw him coming. On at least one occasion, it was reported that he spent six hours confessing the most trivial of transgressions. Still he found no peace.

Finally, in the study of Scripture he discovered God's plan for salvation. The light which broke in his mind was as bright and life changing as that which blinded Paul on the road to Damascus. The experience was recorded in his own words:

> Night and day I pondered until I saw the connection between the justice of God and the statement that "the just shall live by his faith." Then I grasped that the justice of God is that righteousness by which through grace and sheer mercy God justifies us through faith. There upon I felt myself to be reborn and to have gone through open doors into paradise. The whole of scripture took on a new meaning. . . . This passage of Paul became for me a gate to heaven . . . faith leads you in and opens up God's heart and will, that you should see pure grace and overflowing love.[2]

RAYMOND H. BAILEY

Romans 1:17 Faith

The story is told of a little boy who was asked by his father to go upstairs and get the newspaper. The upstairs was dark, and the little fellow was afraid. His father assured him that there was no reason to fear because God was up there in the dark room.

The boy started upstairs with the faith and assurance his father had given him, but as he neared the dark room his fear returned. He got to the door of the dark room and stopped. After some moments he said, "God, since you are already in there, how about throwing the paper out here to me?"

Paul said, "The just shall live by faith." That's easy to say but not always easy to do. There are times in life when our faith falters because of fear, and in those moments we are reassured by Paul's promise.

JAMES A. YOUNG

Romans 1:17 Faith

When God asks us to live by faith, he is not asking us to do anything that we don't already know how to do. We already know how to walk and live by faith. We do it every day. When we buy canned goods at the grocery store, we are trusting that they are not contaminated by a botulism that could kill us. When the prescription is filled by the pharmacist, we trust that he knows what he is doing and will give us the right drug. When the nurse in the hospital gives us an injection, we have to trust that she is giving us the right medicine. When the anesthesiologist comes to put a mask over our face, we are forced to trust that this person is going to give us the right amount of gas to help us sleep rather than the wrong amount of gas which could kill us. We are forced to trust the surgeon who will take the scalpel in hand and make an incision in our bodies. We must trust the pilot who flies the commercial jet liner that we use, and on and on we could go with examples of those areas of life in which we are forced to trust. God is saying to us, "Take that trust you already know how to use and put it in Christ, my Son."

J. DIXON FREE

Romans 1:18-32 The Wrath of God

Many people have a hard time accepting the possibility that God can feel any wrath or anger. They think that God is all love. A close reading of the Scriptures tells us that to reject God's love is to accept God's punishment. The other side of the coin of love is wrath. The options before God are acceptance or rejection. God is not angry and out to punish people. But when people choose to turn against God, God gives people over to themselves. This is "God's wrath." We are so made by God in his image that we are truly human only when free to affirm or deny God, to accept or reject God.

The good news of God in Christ Jesus is that God is for us and wants to redeem us. But at the same time, God will not manipulate us to choose him instead of evil. One of my all-time favorite television programs was "Family Affair." In one episode Sissy was going off to spend the weekend with some hippies without her Uncle Bill's blessing. She was caught up in their declarations of love and freedom. Right before she left, little Buffy spoke with her childlike wisdom the truth that she was glad their Uncle Bill was not a hippy. Because if he had been a hippy, he would not have had time to take care of his family. The hippies talked about love. Their Uncle Bill lived love. Sissy woke up to the truth and stayed home where she knew true love and full freedom. God will give us up—not because he ceases to love us but because he will not force us to love him or obey him. We will never know freedom or joy when we live in the wrath of God we choose for ourselves.

ROBERT W. BAILEY

Romans 1:18-22 Revelation

The question is asked often, "What about the person who has never heard of God? What will happen to him in the day of judgment?" Paul made it clear in Romans that God has revealed himself in the things he has made.

Elizabeth Barrett Browning wrote in *Aurora Leigh*:

> Earth's crammed with heaven,
> And every common bush afire with God;
> But only he who sees, takes off his shoes—
> The rest sit round it and pluck blackberries.

God gives us the power to close our eyes to his revelation if we choose; but if we open our eyes and look at the glories he has created, we will see God in and through them. Paul made it very clear that no person will be able to stand before God and say, "I have an excuse."

JAMES A. YOUNG

Romans 1:18-23 No Escape

In 1975 a group of wealthy people in California who were upset over the world situation paid $12,800 each to form a camp where they could escape the threat of anarchy, nuclear war, or some other catastrophe.

The camp is called Scott Meadows Club and covers 712 acres in the Cascade Mountains near the Oregon border. Members are not allowed to reveal the exact location of the camp, and prospective members are taken there blindfolded.

In spite of annual dues of $3,000, a number of people have been attracted to this doomsday retreat.

There is no such retreat from the doom of God's wrath. No elaborately made plans for survival will avail anyone in the hour of God's judgment. There will be no escape.

HARDY DENHAM

Romans 1:18-32 Judgment

The phrase "God also gave them up" (v. 24) has a dreadful sound, like clods of dirt falling on a coffin. It describes the freedom God gives us in life and eternity. C. S. Lewis once said that in the end there will be only two kinds of people—those who have said to God, "Thy will be done," and those to whom God will say, "Thy will be done." The Lord sorrowfully allows us to go the direction of our choosing.

BILL D. WHITTAKER

Romans 1:20 Seeing the Invisible

On a Friday night, November 8, 1895, Professor Wilhelm Conrad Roentgen, a physicist in Germany, was in his home laboratory working late. He was experimenting with a thin bubble of glass to which were attached a pair of electric wires. On the littered bench were other pieces of equipment: a spark coil, a condenser, and a sheet of cardboard coated with a chemical.

Taking a sheet of heavy black paper, the physicist covered the tube except for a tiny square opening in one end. He shut off the gaslight and turned on the current. And in the darkness he noticed a curious thing—the chemically coated sheet of cardboard was glowing in its own light!

Puzzled, Roentgen picked up the cardboard. And in that instant, something amazing happened. No one knows precisely what occurred, but as Roentgen held that cardboard in his hand, he saw on its surface four dark lines. And he saw that the lines moved as he moved his hand. They bore a perfect resemblance to the bones in his fingers. The scientist sat and looked at the fleshless bones, fearing to remove his hand from the cardboard lest his discovery be only a dream!

The news of the great discovery spread like lightning. Scientists and news reporters came from everywhere to see this strange experiment. Roentgen admitted he was at a loss to explain the phenomenon.

"But what is this ray, Professor?" a reporter insisted. "Is it light? Is it electricity?"

Roentgen shook his head.

"Then how do you explain it?" asked the reporter.

Roentgen hesitated. "I don't know," he said. "X stands for the unknown—the invisible. So I merely call it the X ray."

Paul, the writer of Romans, said the invisible mysteries of the ages are not clearly seen. We cannot explain or fully understand them, except that God has provided us with a spiritual-type X ray to look through the eyes of faith.

JACK GULLEDGE

Romans 1:20 General Revelation

I met John my sophomore year in college. He was from Nigeria. We became good friends. I asked him, "John, tell me how you became a Christian."

John replied, "When I was a little boy, running around in the bush country of Nigeria I knew there was a God. I would stand among the trees and look up at the skies at night and know that someone made this world. I knew there was a God, but I didn't know what to call him. One day Josephine Skaggs, a Southern Baptist missionary, came to our village to teach us children how to read. She taught us how to read the Bible. There I discovered the name of the God who had revealed himself to me through the trees and stars."

Our Father is still in the business of revealing the invisible things of God through creation.

BILL BRUSTER

Romans 1:24-26 Guilt

On a sunny day a stern-faced man stood on a street corner in the busy Chicago loop. As pedestrians hurried by he would lift his right arm, point at someone, and say, "Guilty!" The effect on passing strangers was interesting. They would stare at him, hesitate, look away, and then hurry on. One man turned to a companion and asked, "How did he know?"[3]

Guilt is common to us all. We may be guilty of all kinds of offenses great and small. The good news of the gospel is that forgiveness is possible, through faith in Christ.

ALTON H. MCEACHERN

Romans 1:25-27 Homosexuality

I was an Air Force pilot in World War II stationed in North Africa. When I arrived, the Allied Armies were making their way up the boot of Italy. We made daily flights to Naples, Italy, taking supplies in and wounded soldiers out.

On one occasion I remained overnight in Naples, and the next day I joined a group who was going out to Pompeii to tour the ruins of the ancient city. As we made our way through the ruins, we saw ample evidence of the sins of that city. Engraved on the walls along the narrow streets were life-sized sketches of persons engaged in homosexual acts. Paul wrote the Letter to the Romans about AD 56. The city of Pompeii was destroyed by a volcano about AD 79. These engravings give mute testimony to the fact that Paul was writing about a contemporary problem when he wrote, "Men, leaving the natural use of the woman, burned in their lust one toward another" (v. 27).

The gay society is not new; nor is it an acceptable "alternate life-style." Paul called it what it is: a perversion. It is the result of humans perverting God's truth that a man shall leave father and mother and cleave to his wife, and the two (man and woman) shall become one flesh (Matt. 19:5). As a result of this perversion, "God gave them up unto vile affections" (v. 26). The worst thing God can say to any person is, "Have it your way." Homosexuality is the result of people changing God's truth "into a lie" (v. 25).

JAMES A. YOUNG

Romans 1:26-31 Sin

In verses 26-28 Paul described the sins of the flesh, climaxed by homosexuality. In verses 29-31 he cataloged the sins of the spirit—which can be worse. Sin is universal, and it separates us from God. Sin enslaves people. We become like a fly alighting on sticky flypaper. The fly may say, "My flypaper," but the flypaper could surely say, "My fly!" The wages of sin is death (Rom. 6:23). Sin represents the dark side of human nature.

ALTON H. MCEACHERN

Romans 2:1-3 Judgment

In a group counseling session, the psychologist presented a fictitious case study to several teenage girls. The study contained similarities to actual problems of some girls in the group. During the discussion, an interesting phenomenon occurred. The girls criticized and judged their own faults as presented in the case study. Their comments harshly condemned these traits. Later, the girls expressed surprise when the psychologist told them whom they had really judged.

GAGE MCMAHON

Romans 2:1-11 Humans Have a Choice

"Man is a ship with a conscious rudder . . . which can direct its own movements. The rudder has sent the ship going in one direction. It can send the ship going in another. This capacity for free and conscious self-direction is man's peculiar and defining quality."[4]

These words of Lynn Hough provide a striking metaphor for human choice to sin and human potential to repent and turn to God.

RAYMOND H. BAILEY

Romans 2:7 Immortality

Paul, the apostle, addressed those "who by patient continuance in well-doing seek for glory and honour and immortality, eternal life." It is the quest of the soul to use creative gifts to benefit others in service and love.

When William Faulkner accepted the Nobel Prize in Literature at Stockholm, Sweden, he said:

I believe that man will not merely endure: he will prevail. He is immortal, not because he alone among creatures has an inexhaustible voice but because he has a soul, a spirit capable of compassion and sacrifice and endurance.

The poet's, the writer's duty is to write about these things. It is his privilege to help man endure by lifting his heart by reminding him of the courage and honor and hope and pride and compassion and pity and sacrifice which have been the glory of his past.[5]

JACK GULLEDGE

Romans 3:10-23; 7:15-25 Sin

Several years ago David Brinkley interviewed Ann Landers on his television news magazine. She noted that she received about one million letters each year. Brinkley asked her if she saw a common thread running through the letters—one need, one single question. Without hesitating, Ann Landers answered, "What's wrong with me?" In one way or another, every pastor, every counselor, and even every medical doctor hears the same question. We know something is wrong with us. "Sin!" can be a simplistic answer. But in light of Romans 1—3, sin is complex, deep-rooted, gripping, and pervasive.

W. WAYNE PRICE

Romans 3:13 Tongues of Deceit

Gossip is universal and reveals our neurotic weaknesses and is the mirror of the inner person, according to Dr. Gordon W. Allport, a Harvard psychologist who made an extensive study on the subject. He said, "The type of gossip your neighbor prefers is a pretty reliable index of her fears, frustrations, ambitions, insecurities and guilts."[6]

Researchers have been unable to find any marked difference between the gossip quotient of the male and female; both seem equally eager to gossip. And, a study reveals, it is the busy man or woman rather than the idle one who has more information to swap and therefore gossips most.

The customary justification for gossip is the clique: "Where there's smoke, there's fire." The experts discovered that where there's smoke, there's more generally a liar. Psychologists name three main forms of gossip. The first form is "bogey." It refers to a fabrication of facts to play on imaginary fears to regain social prominence or advantage. A second form is the "wedge." It is defined as a hostile or aggressive gossip designed to divide people, ruin faith, or destroy loyalties. No one will ever know how many marriage problems have been caused or how many reputations have been ruined by wedge drivers. The third form of gossip, according to psychologists, is the "pipe dream." It's born of wishful thinking like a Christmas bonus or the imminent firing of an unpopular boss.

We try to deceive others and in the process deceive ourselves, using this immature method to project onto others the things we don't like in ourselves.

Apparently modern psychologists are discovering what Paul said long ago about projection where the pot calls the kettle black. "With their tongues they have used deceit" (3:13). Paul said, "And thinkest thou this,

O man, that judgest them which do such things, and doest the same, that thou shalt escape the judgment of God?" (Rom. 2:3).

JACK GULLEDGE

Romans 3:17-24 Consistency

We had just come out of the Greek Orthodox Church of the Annunciation in Nazareth. The church is built directly over Mary's well, the traditional place where the angel appeared to Mary to announce the coming birth of Jesus. It is fairly authentic since it is the only water source in Old Nazareth. It still has water. Once Turkish conquerors rode their horses into the church to water them. After that the water was piped out to a well on the street a little way from the church.

The guide at the church was upset. After his explanation of the event and the place, we went to the altar then viewed the well through a grate. As we left, he asked for tips and tried to sell slides and picture postcards. Since an adequate tip had been given already for the group, individuals had been told there was no need to tip him again. The slides did not sell well to our group either. When we left, I saw the guide slam down his packages of slides and utter angry words at us because we had not been more profitable to him.

What a tragedy, I thought. *Here is a Christian and a church who have entirely forgotten their purpose. Their purpose is to tell the story of the birth of Jesus and its meaning to the world. Here the preparation was made for the presence of the Christ in the world. Now all energy and effort is put into protecting a place, a place whose purpose has been forgotten.*[7]

JAMES E. CARTER

Romans 3:19 Individual Accountability

The mass murder of six million Jews during World War II is rightly regarded as one of the greatest crimes in history. It was a crime for which the guilty refused to accept blame. Lieutenant Colonel Adolph Eichmann was in charge of the gestapo's Jewish Evacuation Office. When he was called to account for his crimes in the attempt at genocide, he said regarding his role, "I sensed a kind of Pontius Pilate feeling, for I was free of all guilt." Eichmann said he was merely carrying out orders.

Rudolph Franz Hess, the commandant of the concentration camp at Auschwitz where Jews were exterminated, said, "It didn't occur to me at all that I would be held responsible. You see, in Germany it was understood that if something went wrong, then the man who gave the orders was responsible."

The Bible teaches individual accountability for sin. The law of God places Jews and Gentiles alike under the cover of individual accountability.

HARDY DENHAM

Romans 3:21-31 All Have Sinned

America anxiously awaited the outcome of the fifteen months our fifty-two citizens were held hostage in Iran. Across those months our nation was united in its outrage at the atrocity and our dismay that nothing could be worked out to release them sooner. In spite of all our concern over those captives, I suspect that only a few considered the point made to me by a deacon in North Carolina. Just a short while after their capture, he noted to me one day the grave, united concern over the release of the hostages. Then he questioned how many Christians were concerned about the three billion people in the world who are held captive by sin and the forces of Satan.

I honestly could not tell him that I felt there were many people concerned about this astronomical number of spiritual hostages. After all, most church members do not want to think of sin since they do not want to be considered sinful themselves. To them sin is running a red light, being late for a committee meeting, failing to pay a bill on time, or jaywalking on a vacant street. The majority of church members do not look deep into the sin of their lives. If they give any serious thought to sin, it is usually about "those sinners" who ought to get right with God. Like the first-century Jews, most people within the church are concerned in keeping their religious rules which make them feel righteous because of their good deeds. There is little or no concern given the people who do not know God or who are searching for salvation and liberation. Likewise there is seldom any consideration given to the reality that one's practice of religion may block one from God rather than lead one to Christ's liberating freedom.

Sin does abound, and countless people are in bondage to evil, needing release and liberation desperately. People are hostages to their businesses, to their peers, to changing styles, to indebtedness, clubs, drugs, as well as their families. Most people fail to recognize or admit they are hostages to forces which separate them from God, even people who worship religion and its traditions and thus are isolated from God. All people sin, and sin creates bondage which separates them from God.

ROBERT W. BAILEY

Romans 3:21-26 All Have Sinned

All, Paul said, have missed the true standard of righteousness. It is like the old story of the telephone operators. These operators would listen every day to the whistle at the factory. The whistle would blow promptly at twelve o'clock, and they would set their watches by the sound.

One day it was discovered that the man who blew the whistle at the factory always called at the same hour every day and set his watch by the time he got from the telephone operators. They were setting their time by each other instead of some reliable instrument.

DAVID MATTHEWS

Romans 3:23 Sin

Two engineering students have designed the "Really Me" mirror. They wanted a mirror where people could see themselves as they really are. The "Really Me" mirror may be purchased from a company in Connecticut.

The mirror comes in one standard size, twelve by ten inches. Unlike the conventional mirror that projects a reversed, flattened image, the "Really Me" mirror has depth and shows dimension. The president of the Really Me company claims that persons who look in the new mirror will see how others see them.

A reading of Romans will disclose the true nature of human personality. Paul gave the full dimension of people. The first three chapters of Romans contain a picture of how God sees the human race. The Gentiles are sinners (Rom. 1:18-32). The Jews are sinners (Rom. 2:1-28). Unless there is a doubt, all have sinned. There is none righteous. Romans is the "Really Me" mirror for human nature.

HAROLD T. BRYSON

Romans 3:23 Sin

An analysis of humanity's failure to have the glory promised by God (Ps. 8) usually falls on either the side of the optimist or the pessimist. With a little time, the basic goodness will be seen, or all will be lost. A family had two sons, one an optimist and the other a pessimist. One Christmas the parents sought the help of a therapist. The doctor recommended the parents give the little pessimist every toy he had desired, surely his attitude would be overcome. It was suggested the little optimist be given a shoe box with some horse manure and the fallacy of his eternal optimism would be demonstrated.

On Christmas Day the therapist visited the home to see the results of his recommendation. The little pessimist was surrounded by toys but when asked "How was your Christmas?" he responded with complaints and regrets—pessimism prevailed. The psychiatrist asked the whereabouts of his brother and was directed to the backyard. There the little optimist was seen holding the shoe box and peering behind shrubs and buildings. The therapist asked, "Son, how was your Christmas?" The boy responded—"Great Christmas, the best one I have ever had. I got a pony, if I can just find it!"

Concerning people the Bible is neither pessimistic nor optimistic. The Word is realistic—"All have sinned, and come short of the glory of God."

BILL D. WHITTAKER

Romans 3:23-24 Saved by Grace

A story is told about a man who died and went to heaven. The heavenly gatekeeper explained that all who enter heaven must have earned at least two hundred points while on earth. The man was confident that he would have no trouble; he had been a member of a church for sixty-two years and given thousands of dollars through the church. The gatekeeper gave that achievement one point.

A little troubled, the man continued. He pointed to his life as a faithful husband and father and honest businessman involved in many worthy community projects. The gatekeeper gave him another point.

Finally, in desperation the man acknowledged that if the judging were that difficult, the grace of God was his only hope for heaven. When hearing his conclusion, the gatekeeper gave him 198 points.

Heaven is gained only through the grace of God expressed in the free gift of Jesus Christ through whom we have eternal life.

ERNEST D. STANDERFER

Romans 3:24-25 Cross

The pessimist sees man's sinful condition and puts a period. God puts a comma. This is not the end of the story.

For her part in the murder of Duncan, Lady Macbeth became mentally ill. Macbeth went to the doctor to plead her case:

> Canst thou not minister to a mind diseased,
> Pluck from the memory a rooted sorrow,

Raze out the written troubles of the brain,
And with some sweet oblivious antidote
Cleanse the stuff'd bosom of that perilous stuff
Which weighs upon the heart?

The doctor replied:

Therein the patient
Must minister to himself.[8]

Isn't it wonderful to know that we need not or cannot "minister to ourselves" in the guilt we feel for the wrongs we have committed. But God saw humanity's helpless, hopeless condition and acted in the cross of Christ. Paul reminded us that God set Christ forth on the cross for all ages to see that sin was serious and that his love for people is all encompassing. Jesus Christ came into this world of sin-diseased minds and died that we might be reconciled to God.

JAMES A. YOUNG

Romans 4:16-25 Faith, Hope

Some of the biblical examples of faith arose from what seemed initially hopeless. Abraham was an old man, living on what must have seemed a misunderstood promise that he would father a great nation. Yet he waited. When the son through whom the promise was to be fulfilled was required as a sacrifice, Abraham believed. Perhaps the greatest hope always appears initially to be without possibility.

The community in which I live still cherishes one of our greatest examples of faith. He was President "Buck" Ewell, who reopened the College of William and Mary after the Civil War. He had only two or three professors, a few students, no money, and several buildings badly in need of repair. In 1881 the college was again forced to close. But for seven years, until the year of his death, President Ewell rode from his farm three miles west of Williamsburg to ring the bell in Wren Chapel to mark the beginning of school year that would not be. It was his way of telling the world that the college was, indeed, alive. The bell is rung nowadays by the members of each graduating class at the end of the May semester. They ring the bell in answer to his faith in the college.

W. Wayne Price

Romans 4:25 Our Offenses

A preacher I was visiting told me how he punished his children when they were small. His son and daughter who are in their teens sat in the room with me.

He said, "I kept a stick handy. When one of them would misbehave, I would get the stick. I would tell him or her how much it hurt me for them to do wrong. Then I would tell them that what they had done deserved to be punished. I would say I couldn't stand to punish them and that they would therefore have to give me their punishment. I would give the stick to the misbehaving child and turn my back and tell him how many times he should strike me."

As I listened, I was a little afraid that the psychology of what he had done might not be good. I glanced at his daughter.

She smiled and her voice quivered slightly as she said, "I couldn't stand it when Daddy would make me hit him with the stick. Then he would turn to me with tears in his eyes and reach out his arms to hug me and let me know I was forgiven. I know he loves me. And I'll never do anything to hurt him if I can help it."

Elmer L. Gray

Romans 5:1 Faith

Blondin was a famous French tightrope walker who lived in the latter part of the nineteenth century. Once he strung a tightrope across the Niagara Falls. Before thousands of people, Blondin moved from the Canadian side to the American side. When Blondin stepped on American soil, thousands of people cheered and chanted his name, "Blondin! Blondin! Blondin!"

Blondin quieted the crowd with his raised hand and said, "I am going back across the Niagara Falls on the tightrope, but this time I will carry someone on my shoulders. Do you believe in me?"

The crowd chanted, "We believe! We believe!"

Blondin then asked, "Who will be the person?"

The crowd was silent. Out of the crowd came a man. He climbed on Blondin's shoulders and allowed himself to be taken to the Canadian side of the falls.

Thousands of people had said, "We believe!" But only one really believed. The crowd responded intellectually, but one gave his life to what he believed.

Faith is more than intellectual assent to propositions about God. No, faith is giving yourself to what you believe. Christian faith is opening life to a person and giving yourself to that person, namely Jesus Christ.

HAROLD T. BRYSON

Romans 5:1 Peace

In the War of 1812, Andrew Jackson and his troops defended the city of New Orleans against the British and won the battle. Unknown to Jackson and his men, however, the battle was fought weeks after the peace treaty had already been signed in Europe. But because of the slowness of communications, the troops at New Orleans didn't get the word until it was too late. Soldiers died on either side for a peace that had already been secured.

In Romans 5:1, Paul said that our peace with God has been won for us by Jesus Christ and may be ours through faith. He puts it like this, "Therefore being justified by faith, we have peace with God."

The battle has already been fought, and peace with God has already been made. And it is ours only for the taking.

J. B. FOWLER

Romans 5:1-2 Justification

The movie *Gandhi* received eight Oscars in the 1983 Academy Awards presentation.

It is a magnificent film about the life of the little brown man in a loincloth who single-handedly through the force of moral suasion changed the course of world history. It is an inspiring story of a man. The story of Gandhi always encourages us to know that any person's life can have meaning, that what one person can do is really absolutely fantastic, that moral force and strength really do count in what is often an immoral world.

I do not regularly read the New York *Times*. But once a friend lent me the book review section of a Sunday issue of the New York *Times* so I could read a particular book reviewed.

In this was a review of a then new biography of Mahatma Gandhi. Gandhi without a doubt was one of the world's greatest men. He was truly one of the inspiring and shaping forces of the twentieth century as he virtually single-handedly led India to independence. The question has been asked many times, Was Gandhi a Christian? It is one with which many people have struggled a great deal.

The reviewer of the new Gandhi biography indicated that no one who knew him well ever accused Gandhi of hypocrisy, seriously questioned his motives, or doubted that he was a good man. However, in many ways he never fully faced the twentieth century. India's perennial weakness is that it never produces enough food and goods to create a self-sufficient people. And the population explosion was invented there. But Gandhi advocated self-restraint rather than birth control, cottage handicrafts rather than industry and industrialized agriculture. In these ways he aggravated India's problems. He fought for the "untouchables," but there are now over one hundred million of them, and they are worse off than ever.

The reviewer ended by writing, "The message of Gandhi's life, it seems to me, is that goodness is not enough."

The Bible teaches us that too. It takes more than goodness to make it. It takes Christ. No matter how good a person may have been that does not qualify him to gain entrance into the kingdom of God. Jesus told even Nicodemus that he had to be born again.

Once a young man whom we have called the rich young ruler approached Jesus. He wanted to know what he had to do for eternal life. When Jesus quoted him the second table of the Ten Commandments, he said that he had done that, and he probably had. But that negative goodness was not enough. He needed to shed himself of anything that would hinder his full commitment to Jesus. In his case, it was his fortune.

The apostle Paul expressed it by saying, "Therefore, since we are justified by faith, we have peace with God through our Lord Jesus Christ. Through him we have obtained access to this grace in which we stand, and we rejoice in our hope of sharing the glory of God" (Rom. 5:1-2, RSV).

Goodness is not enough. Gandhi proved that. The Bible witnesses to it. Christ is what we need.

JAMES E. CARTER

Romans 5:1-5 Trouble

Moffatt translates Romans 5:3, "We triumph even in our troubles." This attitude was expressed by a blind businessman in Beaver Dam, Kentucky, when he spoke of his troubles—"I do not think about what I have lost; I'm just thankful for what I still have."

BILL D. WHITTAKER

Romans 5:2 Grace

We have always had a dog around our house. Our family is never complete unless it includes a canine of some description (or often of no adequate description).

Shortly before we moved from Natchitoches, Louisiana, to Alexandria, Louisiana, where I served with the Louisiana Baptist Convention, we had to give our dog away. Since we lived in an apartment for the first three and a half months that turned out to have been fortuitous. Not only were dogs not allowed in the apartment, but Bugger Bear was definitely not cut out for apartment living. In fact, his wandering ways were one factor that caused us to have to find another home for him.

Three days and three rains after we moved into our new house, unsodded yard and all, the children saw an article in the newspaper about the dog pound. So they sallied forth to the pound one rainy afternoon to see the dogs. Thinking they had no money, their mother felt it was safe to allow them to go—just to look.

What their mother did not know was that they had tapped the lunch money fund. In a short while they returned carrying with them the cutest, big eyed, big eared, and big footed, tawny little pooch you will ever hope to see. Supposedly about six weeks of age, he also was supposedly half cocker spaniel and half beagle hound. That has yet to be proved.

Of course, it didn't take but a few minutes for the dog to wiggle his way into our hearts. Tim became a solid and established member of the family.

One cold evening Tim was in the house before the fireplace playing with the children. As I watched him play, giving and receiving affection and personal attention, I thought of how fortunate Tim was. But for one choice, he could still have been in the animal shelter on a cold, wet floor with no personal attention or affection. Life could have been bleak and cold and unpromising for him. Instead it was warm and bright and filled with love.

Then my thoughts moved a step further. This is the very meaning of grace. But for one choice we would be unforgiven, untouched by love, and unaware of our acceptance. God did choose us, however. And through his choice, he has shown us his love through Christ, given us forgiveness of our sins, and accepted us into his family of faith.[9]

James E. Carter

Romans 5:2 Hope of Sharing God's Glory

Hope is confident assurance, according to James W. Cox, who has taught preaching at The Southern Baptist Theological Seminary in Louisville since 1959. In his book *Surprised by God* (Broadman Press, 1979, p. 89), he has a chapter on "Hope Unashamed." In that chapter he tells about D. E. King, a black preacher from Chicago.

Someone asked Pastor King why black Christians were always joyful in their worship, even when things were not going well. The pastor explained, "We rejoice in what we are going to have."

No matter what life's circumstances are, Christians can rejoice. They can rejoice because of what they are going to have. Christians can have the confident assurance that they will share the glory of God.

Hope is counting so much on the good that is to come that you behave today in such a way that you will be ready for tomorrow's blessing.

ELMER L. GRAY

Romans 5:3-5 Trials

The Latin motto of one of the Scottish clans is *"Sub Pondere Cresco"* ("I grow under the burden").

In Romans 5:3-5, the apostle Paul showed us how Christians, rightly using their problems and burdens, can grow in Christ's likeness. He introduced this strange concept with equally strange words: "We glory in tribulations also: knowing that tribulation worketh patience" (v. 3).

Harry Emerson Fosdick, one of America's preachers of an earlier generation, preached for many years in New York City. In one of Fosdick's books, he tells about an apple grower who lived in the apple-bearing section of the state of Maine.

One of Fosdick's friends told the preacher about a visit he made to that section of Maine on one occasion. He saw apple trees so loaded down with fruit that their branches had to be propped up to keep them off the ground. When he asked the apple grower why those particular trees were so loaded with fruit, the apple grower told the man to look at the trunks of the trees near the ground.

Looking at the trunks of the trees, the man noticed that the tree had been severely wounded with deep gashes that had healed over. The apple grower then explained the reason for the gashes:

"We have discovered that when an apple tree begins to run to wood and leaves and not to fruit," the man said, "that if we will gash it deeply it will almost always produce more apples. We don't know everything about how it works, but we know that the more the tree is bruised the more it seems to produce."

In Romans 5:3-5, Paul showed us the same thing: suffering in the life of a yielded believer produces a character of the highest quality.

J. B. FOWLER

Romans 5:3-5 Experience

Paul pointed out that difficult experiences bring a maturing patience and hope. Some of life's greatest lessons are learned by trial and error. This kind of wisdom comes from years of experience.

"Uncle Zeke," a quaint character in Kentucky, was known for this kind of wisdom. One day a young man asked him, "Uncle Zeke, how come you're so wise?"

"Because I've got good judgment," the old man replied. "Good judgment comes from experience, and experience—well, that comes from poor judgment!"

JACK GULLEDGE

Romans 5:5 Burdens

Bishop Lattimer was a quaint, peculiar bishop of the church. One day while he was visiting a man, the man confessed, "Bishop, I have never had to bear a cross."

His confession shocked the bishop. Quickly jumping to his feet, the bishop sharply commanded: "Get my horse; I am sure that God is not where there is no cross! Get my horse!"

You can count on this: God is where the crosses are the heaviest. Where the trials are the severest and the night is the darkest, there God delights to be.

In Romans 5:5, Paul eluded to this when he declared that in the midst of our severest trials "the love of God is shed abroad in our hearts by the Holy Ghost which is given unto us."

Behind the darkest storm cloud the sun still shines.

J. B. Fowler

Romans 5:6-8 Worth Dying For

William Barclay, in his commentary on Luke, told a story about a wandering scholar in the Middle Ages. Old Muretus took ill and landed in a hospital for the poor. The doctors stood over him discussing his case in Latin, never dreaming that the old man understood every word. They suggested to one another that since he was a worthless wanderer, they could use him for medical experimentation. The old scholar looked up and spoke to them in Latin, "Call no man worthless for whom Christ died."[10]

W. Wayne Price

Romans 5:8 Cross

Years ago, Arnold Toynbee wrote ten large volumes concerning the history of humanity. Throughout this multivolume work, he traced the rise and fall of civilization after civilization. Toynbee assessed why these civilizations rose and fell with such regular monotony. He concluded that a civilization may survive according to religious response to dangerous situations.

In one of his works, Toynbee described a dream he had had years before. This dream made a strong impression on him. He dreamed that he was in Ampleforth in Yorkshire, England. Above the altar a huge cross was suspended. He saw himself clinging to the foot of the cross, and he heard a voice saying, "*Amplexus, expecta*" (Cling and wait). Toynbee gave a message by urging people to cling to the cross.

HAROLD T. BRYSON

Romans 5:8 Atonement

In Christian theology there are a number of theories of the atonement. It may be viewed as a ransom. Surely, the cross and resurrection represent God's victory over sin and evil. This view is called "*Christus Victus*." The cross has had a great moral influence on humanity as well. The most popular view of the atonement is that Christ was our vicarious substitute on the cross. He paid our sin debt.

Dr. E. Y. Mullins once taught at and was president of The Southern Baptist Theological Seminary in Louisville, Kentucky. He would lecture in class on Christ's atoning death. Then he would say, "If there had been only one sinner in the world, and if his name were Edgar Young Mullins, Christ would still have come; Christ would still have died!"

ALTON H. MCEACHERN

Romans 5:8 God's Desperate Love

Graham Greene's novel *The Heart of the Matter* is about a white police official in a British colony in Africa who becomes involved in a web of intrigue, a sordid affair with a woman, and finally the murder of a trusted assistant. Henry Scobie, the police official, reaches the point that he cannot live with his guilt and despair. He decides to take his own life. But before carrying out his plan, he decides to go to church one last time. His purpose in doing so is more to curse God than to pray. But in the sanctuary, there suddenly breaks in on Scobie the awareness of a God who will not let him go. This amazing persistence causes him to cry out, "How desperately God must love me!"

Even though God will allow a man to go on in his sin past a point of no return, he loves the sinner so desperately that he gave Christ to die, so that the door of salvation could be open.

HARDY DENHAM

Romans 5:10 Reconciled

Two eminent theologians, Emil Brunner and Karl Barth, did not always agree on matters of theology. At one time Barth publicly denounced one of Brunner's theological positions. Shortly before Brunner died, however, he received a message from Barth: "Commended to our God, even by me." Barth explained that the time had long passed when he thought he had to say no to Brunner, especially since we all live only by virtue of the fact that a great and merciful God has said yes to us.

God did not turn his back on us though we were sinners. Through Christ he has said yes and made us his friends.

ERNEST D. STANDERFER

Romans 5:19*b* When One Is More

Our day is characterized by staggering statistics. Everything seems to eventually get counted, measured, or averaged. The human brain supposedly contains one trillion cells. Weighed by tons, it takes a 22-number figure to calculate the earth's weight. Have you heard of the googol? It is a figure followed by 100 zeroes.

While our attempts to unravel the universe's mysteries compel us to use such statistics, the Bible reminds us of the importance of one, especially when that one is Jesus Christ. Only through Christ do we discover salvation and enter a right relationship with God. When one is Christ, it is more than any set of mathematical statistics, whatever their magnitude or meaning.

ERNEST D. STANDERFER

Romans 5:20 Abounding Grace

Ernest Gordon, in his book *Through the Valley of the Kwai,* told of a young soldier in a jungle prison hospital dying of cerebral malaria. He had had to shoot a man suspected of collaborating with the enemy. In his delirium the soldier shouted, "Of course, I had to kill him. There was nothing else to do. But before I shot him through the head, he looked at me, his eyes pleading with mercy. He cannot forgive me; his wife cannot forgive me; nobody can forgive me."

Paul wrote that where sin abounds with its accompanying burden of intolerable guilt, grace also abounds. In other words, where the river of sin runs wide and deep, the grace of God runs wider and deeper.

HARDY DENHAM

Romans 6:1-4 Newness

Perhaps the most nostalgic time of year comes on New Year's eve. It bids both a look backward on an old year filled with mistakes and a leap forward to an optimistic hope for a happier year.

Yet, other times during the year invite fresh beginnings: Easter, signaling the ever-new reality of eternal life in Christ; summer, marking the passage of school children into new adventures for a few months; September, ushering in a new school year for students of all ages; and Advent, heralding a new beginning of the Christian year through the celebration of Christ's birth.

Going ahead into newness of life invites the discarding of negative aspects of former things and permits the full enjoyment of fresh challenges.

GAGE MCMAHON

Romans 6:3 Baptized unto Death

For many years I have told baptismal candidates that standing in the baptismal waters with hands folded across the chest was an ancient symbol of death. I have explained that such a symbol signifies their faith that Jesus died for them. I had no proof of the validity of that symbol. While visiting the Smithsonian in Washington, DC, I saw an Egyptian mummy that had been preserved from 4000 BC. The mummy was wrapped with his hands across his chest as a symbol of death. It dawned upon me that folded hands as a symbol of death was at least 6000 years old. Paul's words took on added significance.

BILL BRUSTER

Romans 6:4-5 Potential

Imagine if you will two watermelon seeds lying side by side. One of those seeds is the real thing while the other is an exact duplicate of a watermelon seed. It was created by a scientist. It has the same amount of moisture in it as the real seed. The chemical makeup of the duplicate is the same as the real watermelon seed. But if we planted both of those seeds what would we get? First of all, the seed made by the scientist would lie in the ground and would deteriorate and disappear into the earth. The seed made by God would also deteriorate; but as it was deteriorating—dying to self—it would put up a sprout that would become under the right conditions a watermelon vine, and upon that watermelon vine would grow several watermelons. Each of these melons would have several hundred seeds in it. Each of those seeds in those melons would have the potential for doing the same thing in the future. You see, there is more potential in that one watermelon seed than the human mind can even comprehend. That's the way it is with the potential of the Christian life through the power of Jesus Christ.

J. Dixon Free

Romans 6:6 Restored to the Divine Image

"Beauty and the Beast" is the story of a man who traded his humanity for material possessions. The beast was a man whose greed had brought a curse upon him and reduced him to an animal existence. Horrible in appearance, he lived in beautiful surroundings. At night he foraged for his food with the beasts of the field. His only hope for restoration was to be loved by a creature of beauty. There was a beauty whose compassion transcended natural repugnance to ugliness and motivated her to sacrifice herself in love for the beast. The result was a metamorphosis of the beast to his original image.

Is this not a parable of every human being created in the image of God and corrupted by sin? The love of Christ in spite of our ugliness and meanness has made it possible for us to be beautiful children of God.

Raymond H. Bailey

Romans 6:6-9 Regeneration

If you take a pig from the pigpen and spruce him all up with bows on his ears and on his tail, wash him good and spray him with the best of perfume, and then let him out in the yard, what do you think that pig is going to do? Not only will he try to find a mud puddle but if he doesn't have one he will try to make one because that is his nature. On the other hand, if you take a little lamb and throw that lamb in the mud puddle, you will find that it will drag itself out because its nature is not to live in the mud.

J. DIXON FREE

Romans 6:11 Baptism

Baptism is a demarcation. It marks a dividing line in the life of a Christian. Baptism symbolizes our death to sin and self, burial with Christ, and resurrection to a new life.

Prior to the battle of the Alamo, Texas commander Travis drew a saber-thin line across the floor of the chapel. He challenged his men to step across that line and die for Texas. All but one did.

Christian baptism is a symbol of the believer's decision which means death and new life.

ALTON H. MCEACHERN

Romans 6:12-23 Sin

An observer, one freezing winter day, noticed a bird of prey light upon a floating carcass in the Niagara River below Buffalo. As the bird fed on the carcass, it was aware of the great falls near at hand, but it planned to fly away before it reached the dangerous point. When the thunder of the falls was near, the giant bird stretched its wings to fly away from the imminent danger. But it was too late. The bird's talons had frozen to the carcass it had been feeding on. He was swept over the rapids with the creature to which he was attached. How often we are destroyed by habits and sins which we thought we could control or stop anytime we wanted to. To commit one's self to the way of sin is to be carried along its path. When we yield ourselves to Christ, we are under his dominion and free from the slavery of sin.

WILLIAM P. TUCK

Romans 6:13 Instruments of Righteousness

Suzanne Roberts, of Tempe, Arizona, strolled casually into an auction house fifteen years ago during a visit to New Orleans. She bid fifteen dollars for an old violin. The dealer who sold it to her said that it was probably worth at least seventy-five dollars.

Recently she read in the local paper of an expert appraiser of musical instruments who'd moved to the city. She took the violin to him for an appraisal. After careful study, he told her that her violin dated 1760 was a genuine Tomasso Carcassi, a famous eighteenth-century violin maker of the Cremona school, home of Guarnerius, Stradivarius, and Amati violins.

The appraiser told Suzanne Roberts that the rare musical instrument is easily worth $140,000 and probably more if she can have the appropriate repairs done by an expert.[11]

Violins can look much alike to the untrained eye. But expert appraisers know the difference when the maker is a master at his craft. The apostle Paul pointed out this truth in spiritual terms. We can be instruments of little worth until we're made and molded by the Master's hand, and then we become instruments of righteousness and great value.

JACK GULLEDGE

Romans 6:19 Total Surrender

Throughout his notable ministry, William Booth, founder of the Salvation Army, majored on ministering to people who had made nothing out of their lives. He gathered a virtual army of human derelicts and wanderers from the gutters of London and introduced them to Christ and a new way of life. When asked how he did it, he replied, "I don't know; all I know is that Jesus Christ has had all there is of me."

This total surrender undoubtedly explains much of God's blessings on his ministry. It illustrates what God does through those entirely yielded to him.

ERNEST D. STANDERFER

Romans 6:22 Freedom

I did it again.

You don't know how I hate to admit it, but I locked myself out of the house again. This time I was headed for a morning speaking engagement. As I was rushing out of the house, I saw one domestic chore I was supposed to have done early that morning. Putting down my New Testament, my speech, and my keys, I performed my task. Then I rushed by, picking up the Testament and the speech but missing the keys. As I pulled the back door shut behind me, I realized that I did not have my keys. In trying to keep the house safe from thieves and robbers, we had removed the key that once was hid outside the house. I was outside. The keys were inside.

I called the church office. My rescuer came out and picked me up. Just as we drove into the church driveway that car died, unwilling to start again. Counting my own car that I could not drive because the keys were locked in the house, it took me three cars to get to my speaking engagement. I breathlessly arrived just in time to walk straight to the platform. Fortunately they had some preliminaries during which I caught my breath before delivering myself of that speech.

Upon returning to the office, I found the following piece of poetry by a yet unnamed poet:

> There once was a preacher named Carter
> Who couldn't keep keys where he oughter.
> Locked out of his house,
> He felt like a louse;
> You'd think after twice he'd be smarter!

Don't you, indeed, think he would be smarter? It reminds me of the plaque I have seen many times before with the legend, "We get too soon old and too late smart."

But run back over your life and think of some of those things about which you should have been smarter. The nature of sin is that we are condemned to repeating the same sins, doing the same things over and over again.

There is a temptation to which you have succumbed time and time again.

There is an attitude in which you have persisted through the years.

There is a weakness to which you have given in more than once.

There is an emotion—anger, perhaps, or jealousy—that keeps cropping up in your life.

There is the way that you continue to act little and petty when you should be big and gracious.

There is that stance, that pattern, that habit, that life-style that just seems too much to break.

These are things that we do again and about which we feel like a louse. You would think we would be smarter. It isn't a matter of intelligence but grace. You already know better; it is a matter of doing better.

And we are given hope for this by the gospel. Listen: "But now you have been set free from sin and are the slaves of God. Your gain is a life fully dedicated to him, and the result is eternal life" (Rom. 6:22, GNB).

JAMES E. CARTER

Romans 6:23 The Wages of Sin

A common adage of the day is: if people could achieve the freedom they wanted, they could get their lives together and have the fulfillment they desire. Their struggle to be free is bound up in their effort to be or make their own god, and thus they always fail. They inevitably wind up like the ancient Greek legendary figure Sisyphus. This mythical character was the son-in-law of Atlas and the father of Odysseus. During his life he craftily used and abused many women. Upon his death he was given severe punishment for his sins—he had to roll a large stone in Hades to the top of a hill. The stone immediately rolled down, and Sisyphus had to begin again. Over and over and over again Sisyphus had to go through the tortuous task of rolling the stone up the hill, never able to complete the task or rest.

People today seem endlessly to be doing the same things over and over again—even good things—but getting nowhere. They begin with optimism at the bottom of the hill, thinking that their legalism, conformity, or religious tradition will somehow provide them passage beyond the bonds of sin. But their way apart from God never does quite succeed. The inescapable truth is all of us sin—regardless of how religious we may appear. And the basic failure of human sin is founded on the biblical truth that sin is rebellion against God at its very core! And the wages of sin is death!

ROBERT W. BAILEY

Romans 6:23*b* God's Free Gift

After being driven by a severe storm years ago, a ship was powerless and far from any port. With all their supplies exhausted or destroyed, the crew was fainting from thirst. Finally when another ship came into sight, they cried out, "Water! Water!"

The answer quickly came back, "You have only to draw water from the ocean. You are surrounded by fresh water!" Only then did the crew realize they were off the coast of Brazil where the Amazon River pushes fresh, living water a hundred miles out into the Atlantic!

Sometimes we may feel so burdened and overwhelmed by our sin that we feel God has forsaken or ignored us. The truth is all we have to do is request and receive God's amazing grace and eternal life in Christ Jesus! It is a free gift, something which we cannot do or achieve on our own. So long as we try to eradicate our sins and solve our problems on our own, we will drift aimlessly on the perishing vessels of life crying out for rescue and relief. When we decide to allow God in Christ Jesus to deal with our sin, then through our confession and Christ's forgiveness, we can experience God's free gift of pardon and life eternal.

ROBERT W. BAILEY

Romans 6:23 Judgment

Charles Finney, the great evangelistic preacher who rocked the United States with his evangelistic message, told of his conversion experience. He was in law school nearing time for completion of his course of study when on one occasion he was left alone in a law office and came under a certain thought pattern that led him to Jesus Christ. As he sat alone in this office the Lord began to deal with him. It seemed that the Lord was saying to him, "Finney, what are you going to do when you finish your course of study?"

Finney's answer was, "I'll put out a shingle and practice law."

It seemed that the voice of the Lord came back and said, "Then what are you going to do?"

Finney's answer to the Lord was, "Then I'll get rich."

The piercing word of God came back to him, "Then what are you going to do?"

Finney replied in his heart, "Lord, then I'll retire and take it easy."

The word came back from God and asked him again, "What then, Finney?"

Finney's answer was, "Then I'll die Lord."

Finally, the Lord said to Finney in his heart, "Then what, Finney?"

And the words that came in Finney's mind were, "Then the judgment will come, Lord." Charles Finney ran out into the woods alone convicted of the fact that he, a lawyer, was going one day to have to stand before the judgment bar of God and be judged, and he knew he was convicted. He knew he was going to receive the just sentence from God. This led Finney to repentantly accept Jesus Christ as his Savior.[12]

J. DIXON FREE

Romans 7:6 Spirit and Flesh

In the writings of Frenchman Blaise Pascal we find this assessment of human nature: "It is dangerous to show man too often that he is equal to beasts, without showing him his greatness. It is also dangerous to show him too frequently his greatness without his baseness. It is yet more dangerous to leave him ignorant of both. But, it is very desirable to show him the two together."

W. WAYNE PRICE

Romans 7:12 Law Is Good

In a preschool Sunday School department, a little boy was disturbing everyone. He made an ugly face at one child, pinched another, and snatched a paper away from another.

A worker shook her head at him, touched a finger to her lips, and motioned for him to be quiet and be good. He whirled around and shoved yet another child.

The worker hurried to him, smiled at him, and led him away from the others. She sang a little song for him and then told him how good it was to do things for others and to make them happy. Then she asked him to help her share the cookies. Very carefully, the little boy made certain that every child received a cookie and a napkin.

When the period was over, he came to the worker and smiled widely. He had turned from being a little devil to being a little angel.

He said, "Thank you for helping me be good."

The teacher laughed happily and patted him on the head.

Law is like that teacher. It is to guide us in doing good. But law isn't a person and, therefore, it can't motivate us as the teacher motivated that church. Law is good, but only Christ can help us obey it for the good of everyone.

ELMER L. GRAY

Romans 7:13-25 Struggle

Biblical scholars are divided about the meaning of these verses. Some are convinced that Paul was writing about his preconversion state while others are equally convinced that Paul was discussing the Christian life. Whatever the case, we are all aware that a struggle goes on in our hearts as we attempt to live the Christian life. At times Christ has the upper hand, and at times we allow Satan to rule our lives.

Milton contrasts the mind of Christ with the mind of Satan in *Paradise Lost*. Satan's attitude is expressed in the words:

> The mind is its own place, and in itself
> Can make a Heaven of Hell, a Hell of Heaven.
> What matter where, if I be still the same,
> And what I should be, all but less than he
> Whom thunder hath made greater? Here at least
> We shall be free; the Almighty hath not built
> Here for his envy, will not drive us hence:
> Here we may reign secure; and, in my choice,
> To reign is worth ambition, though in Hell:
> Better to reign in Hell than serve in Heaven.[13]

God has given us the power of choice. The struggle we face in the Christian life is the result of our own failure to be "filled with the Spirit." My own struggle to live according to God's will and purpose for my life convinces me that Paul was writing about his struggle as a Christian.

JAMES A. YOUNG

Romans 7:15 Doing the Thing I Love-Hate

Daniel Yankelovich in an article in *Psychology Today* reported a modern vignette of a person trapped in a cycle of acknowledged self-destructive behavior.

A patient told her psychotherapist that she was worn out though she had not reached her thirtieth birthday. Her life in the fast lane was getting to be too much for her. Too many parties, too much sex, too much booze, and too much pleasure had left her exhausted.

"Why don't you stop?" her psychologist asked.

She paused for a moment stunned by the obvious question. Her startled expression turned to enlightenment as she exclaimed: "You mean I really don't have to do what I want to do?"[14]

Perhaps the greatest mystery of sin is why a person continues to do that which produces only misery and self-destruction.

RAYMOND H. BAILEY

Romans 7:19-25 Maintaining Direction

Wilfred Grenfell, a noted missionary, had just received a new boat for his work in Labrador. A woman called one night asking for his help, for she was gravely ill. Several assistants went with him in order to make the trip to minister to this woman. They had traveled some time through the darkness when they realized they were going in the wrong direction. In order to save their lives on the perilous sea, they would have to run the boat aground, destroying it. As a result the woman died before Grenfell was able to get to her, and he almost lost his life. A subsequent investigation revealed that the workman in the boat factory in Liverpool had dropped the brass screw used to attach the compass to the boat. Instead of taking the time to look for and find that essential screw, the worker picked up another one—a steel screw. This steel screw had enough magnetic pull on the compass that it threw the boat completely off course, resulting in its destruction.

Even we who are in Christ have a difficult time maintaining our direction, as Paul so vividly testified. We can allow our consciences and our lives to be pulled off course when money, pleasure, ambition, sex, jealousy, hatred, prejudice, spite, or other powerful forces are allowed so near the center of our lives that our integrity is destroyed. In and of ourselves, we do not have enough power and strength to deliver ourselves from the domination of sin. But we can, like Paul, search for our deliverance and find our answer in the strong Son of God, even Jesus Christ our Lord! He can free us from the grips of sin and enable us to maintain our direction as his followers, servants, and disciples.

ROBERT W. BAILEY

Romans 7:24-25 Deliverance

Ernest Gordon entitled his autobiography *Miracle on the River Kwai*. He was a British Highland soldier captured by the Japanese during World War II. The prisoners of war were forced to build a railroad in the jungle. Gordon nearly starved and became the victim of unspeakable tropical diseases. He was not a Christian when he was placed in the death house and left to die.

A fellow prisoner took Gordon out, shared his meager food with him, and nursed him back to health. This friend also introduced Gordon to Christ. Later, as chaplain at Princeton University, Ernest Gordon wrote that the incarnation means Christ "comes into our Death House, to lead us through it."

ALTON H. MCEACHERN

Romans 7:24-25 Our Weakness—His Strength

Leo Tolstoy was one of the greatest novelists in history. His monumental novel *War and Peace* continues to hold a place among the greatest literary works in the world. The early years of Tolstoy's life were spent in sinful living. He was not comfortable with his reprobate life-style and sought ways to be free of it. However, all attempts to reform his life failed. Vices he sought to conquer made him their victim. Once he wrote about the seductive voices that lured him to sin: "I knew where these voices came from. I knew they were destroying my happiness; I struggled, I lost. I fell asleep dreaming of fame and women. . . . It was stronger than I."

Tolstoy's experience is, in general, the experience of every man. All of us have experienced the pull that was stronger than us. We have struggled and lost. But Christ is the victor, and in his strength we find victory over the downward pull that destroys.

HARDY DENHAM

Romans 8:1 Not Guilty

When a person comes under investigation for an alleged crime, authorities may interview the suspect's employer, his relatives, friends, neighbors, and even casual acquaintances. The most innocuous questions, the mere fact of the investigation, can create suspicion of criminality. But what if the suspicion is unfounded and the person is innocent? A grand jury may not indict him, but the accusation will often remain, damage, and sometimes even destroy the suspect.

Reasoning that such innocent people deserve a better deal, District Attorney Henry Wenzel of Suffolk County, New York, has begun a policy of writing official letters to former suspects, stating that they have been totally cleared. What's more, the district attorney's office will send the letter to an employer, or to anyone the innocent party designates, and also incorporate the record of investigation. The letter declares that the suspect was not condemned. But to those of us who know Jesus, we have been declared not guilty by a much higher authority.

BILL BRUSTER

Romans 8:1-11 The Recurrence of Sin

In the disturbing novel *The Plague* by Albert Camus, a French port town of Oran, on the Algerian Coast, was shut off from the rest of the world by a plague. The Black Death moved in its haunted agony across the city, leaving behind its anguish of cruelty, pain, grief, and countless victims. Dr. Rieux, the town's physician, observed the outward and inward responses of the plague-stricken people and concluded that "there are more things to admire in men than to despise." In the awareness that the battle against the plague is a never-ending conflict, Dr. Rieux looked at the joyous crowd after the quarantine had been lifted and observed that "joy is always imperiled."

"He knew what those jubilant crowds did not know but could have learned from books: that the plague bacillus never dies or disappears for good; that it can lie dormant for years and years in furniture and linen-chests; that it bides its time in bedrooms, cellars, trunks, and bookshelves; and that perhaps the day will come when, for the bane and the enlightening of men, it will rouse up its rats again and send them forth to die in a happy city."[15]

Just as there is a never-ending battle against infectious disease, there is a continuous struggle against the recurrence of sin. The war against sin must be waged ceaselessly. Sin will lift its ugly head in many ways and places, but we live with the awareness that it is not by our strength alone but by the grace and power of God which gives us the victory.

WILLIAM P. TUCK

Romans 8:2 Freedom

Nearly four of five Americans don't know what the First Amendment is all about, according to a special Gallup poll measuring freedoms granted under this provision.

George Gallup, Jr., told 285 delegates attending a two-day First Amendment Congress held near Independence Hall, where Congress adopted the ten amendments known as the Bill of Rights in 1790, that 76 percent of a national sample of 1,523 adults drew a blank when asked to define the amendment. It guarantees freedoms of religion, speech, assembly; the right to petition the government for a redress of grievances and a free press.

Paul, the apostle, reminded Christians of their "bill of rights" and responsibilities. While we're free from the law of sin and death, we are to walk in the Spirit. May we not be guilty of forgetting our freedoms but rather using them for the glory of God.

JACK GULLEDGE

Romans 8:5-8 Spiritual Death

To stay long on the ways of the world (or "the flesh") leads eventually to spiritual insensitivity and death. In 1968, Edwin T. Dahlberg told of a friend who had a son in Vietnam. The young man was a member of the Black Berets, an even more specialized force than the Green Berets.

It was the responsibility of this soldier to go far back of the enemy lines at night, often in remote areas where he was not heard from for weeks at a time. He carried only three weapons—a pistol, a knife, and a wire.

Because his work was to be done in complete silence, the pistol was used only as a last resort. The wire was for garroting the enemy around the throat from behind. The knife was for stabbing him to death. The blade was made of such special metal that it had to be shipped back to the United States for sharpening.

Dahlberg said to the father, "Your son is on a very dangerous assignment."

The father replied, "He is; but what I dread most is what this will do to his soul."

David Matthews

Romans 8:11 Power

John Hyde boarded a ship to go from England to India to serve as a missionary. As he walked on the ship, he received a telegram: "John Hyde, are you filled with the Spirit of God?" The message angered him. He crumpled the paper and put it in his pocket. "The audacity of somebody to ask me that question," he said to himself. "Here I am a missionary, sincere, dedicated, leaving my home, going to another country. And someone has the nerve to ask me, 'Are you filled with the Holy Spirit?'"

After awhile, the message of the telegram sunk into his heart, and John Hyde became convicted. He fell upon his knees and cried, "O God, the audacity of me to think that I could pray or preach or witness or live or serve or do anything in my own strength and in my own power. Lord, fill me with your Spirit so I might have power to serve."

John Hyde became one of the greatest missionary statesmen of all time because he realized the truth of what Paul wrote to the Romans: "If the Spirit of him who raised Jesus from the dead dwells in you, he who raised Christ Jesus from the dead will give life to your mortal bodies also through his Spirit which dwells in you" (RSV).

BRIAN L. HARBOUR

Romans 8:14-17 Children of God

The Ugly Duckling is a fascinating children's story with an important lesson about identity. A false self-image caused the ugly duckling a great deal of pain. He didn't know who he was. Attempts to discover his identity and be accepted brought rejection and low self-esteem. The story of his identity crisis has been read to and by children for generations. He had the misfortune to be born into the wrong family. From the beginning, it was obvious he was a misfit. He didn't look like the others. He didn't quack like them, and they wanted nothing to do with him. His mother was ashamed of him and drove him away.

His search for family led to a whole series of rejections. The chickens wouldn't have him, and he couldn't keep up with the wild geese. In utter disdain he found himself isolated and defeated. Finally, one day he came upon the most beautiful creatures he had ever seen. Their color was pure like fresh snow. They moved across the water with poetic motion that could only be described as graceful. He moved in for a closer look. When he looked into the mirror of the water that was their home, he saw his image in the water. To his amazement, he realized that his image was the same as the beautiful creatures he admired. He was not an ugly duckling but a beautiful swan.

The pilgrimage of the swan was not unlike that of the person who tries to be what he is apart from God. Sin gives to humans a distorted image of who they are. They try to behave like something less than they are and suffer because of the false image. Only the discovery of Jesus Christ can reveal to them the beauty that lies within them. He is the mirror that will reflect to the seeker his or her true image.

RAYMOND H. BAILEY

Romans 8:15-16 Papa

Somewhere in the extensive writings of Joachim Jeremias, he tells about an experience in a Near East airport. As he stepped off the airplane, he watched a little Arabic boy run to his father, crying out, "Abba! Abba! Abba!" Jeremias understood what Paul meant when he spoke of the intimacy of sonship whereby we may address God as, "Papa." It is not the emotion of fear or of bondage but of the freedom of belonging to the parent, the household. It is the most intimate relationship with the Heavenly Father.

W. WAYNE PRICE

Romans 8:15-16 Father

Jesus' favorite name for God was "Abba," Father. This was a child's term of endearment for his father. As a boy, Jesus spoke of being about his Father's business. In the midst of his ministry he said, "My Father works, and I work" (see John 5:17). On the cross he prayed, "Father, into thy hands I commit my spirit" (Luke 23:46).

To call God "Father" recognizes him as our Protector (Ps. 23). And it means that God is approachable. Above all, this term means that God cares for us. God is the Father of all humanity by creation and providential care. He is the Father of all believers by adoption. And he is uniquely the Father of Jesus. God's fatherhood becomes the pattern for human fathers.

ALTON H. MCEACHERN

Romans 8:16-17 Self-Worth

Willie Davis from Alabama was one of many football players whom Vince Lombardi helped to achieve success on the gridiron. Although Willie was not a well-known college player, Vince Lombardi took a chance on him, and Willie came through.

When Lombardi was dying of cancer in a hospital in Washington, DC, Willie Davis flew from California to see him. After only a brief visit, Willie left and flew back to the West Coast. Five days later he served as one of the pallbearers at Lombardi's funeral at Saint Patrick's Cathedral in New York City. When the reporters heard that this was Willie's second trip across the country in a week, they asked him why he'd come the first time. After all, everyone knew that Lombardi couldn't live long. Why didn't Willie Davis just wait until his death? In response, Willie said, "Listen, man, I had to come. You see, Mr. Lombardi was the first man who ever made me feel like I was somebody!"

This was the testimony Paul gave about Jesus Christ: he helps us to know that we are somebody. "The Spirit Himself bears witness with our spirit that we are children of God, and if children, heirs also, heirs of God and fellow-heirs with Christ" (NASB).

BRIAN L. HARBOUR

Romans 8:17-21 Love

Walter is the family prodigal in Lorraine Hansberry's *Raisin in the Sun*. He gambles away his sister's college fund, and she gives up on him. Their mother reminds her that relationships must be cultivated, and she pleads for the sister to love Walter. The girl screams out her resentment by suggesting that there is nothing left to love. But the wise mama counsels, "There's always something left to love. And if you ain't learned that, you ain't learned nothin."

W. WAYNE PRICE

Romans 8:18 Glory

In a little church in the far south of Ireland, every window but one is of painted glass. Through that single exception may be seen a breathtaking view: a lake of deepest blue, studded with green islets, backed by range after range of purple hills. Under the window is the inscription: "The heavens declare the glory of God; and the firmament showeth his handiwork" (Ps. 19:1).

As beautiful as some scenic wonders of nature may be, they "are not worthy to be compared with the glory which shall be revealed in us," Paul said.

JACK GULLEDGE

Romans 8:18-30 The Importance of Prayer

Prayer is frequently misunderstood and always difficult, for "prayer is a language embracing more than words, for words are the tools of the mind. The disciplined life or prayer used the combined resources of body, mind, and spirit to realize the possibilities of living."[16]

Prayer is the language the spiritual person develops to communicate with God. A purpose of prayer is to release us from our frailness and limitations to become open to the power and presence of God. A hot air balloon cannot ascend until its sandbags are untied. No matter how much gas is fed into the balloons through the burner, it is held to the ground by the weight of the sandbags. Set free, it can soar into the atmosphere. Prayer can set us free to find the gifts God's Spirit offers us.

Paul assured us that we are not entering into the experience of prayer alone but that in our weakness and lack of understanding, "the Spirit himself intercedes for us with sighs too deep for words" (v. 26, RSV). Through the discipline of prayer, we develop the roots and strength that sustain us in our life of growth and service in Christ. The Japanese grow dwarf trees. Cherry, apple, and other trees never grow more than twelve to eighteen inches tall. They contain the tree by cutting its tap root. The tree can live by its surface roots, but it cannot grow. When we who are in Christ omit prayer from our lives, we cannot grow. We may exist, but we cannot grow. Life will have no joy or vitality, no stirring trumpets in the morning or no calming songs at night when we do not pray.

ROBERT W. BAILEY

Romans 8:24-25 Hope

Viktor Emil Frankl was a Jewish psychologist from Vienna, Austria, who was imprisoned in Auschwitz, a German concentration camp, during World War II. Frankl observed his fellow prisoners and evaluated their outlook on the austerities of being prisoners. Frankl saw many prisoners who faced the circumstances with pessimism. These prisoners generally gave up the struggle for survival and resigned themselves to death. Frankl observed some prisoners who triumphed over the tragic conditions. These prisoners refused to resort to pessimism. They held tenaciously to an optimistic hope. They emerged from their imprisonment and assumed meaningful lives at the end of the war.

Frankl gave much time and thought evaluating the difference between the two types of prisoners. He wrote much of his evaluations in his celebrated book, *Man's Search for Meaning: An Introduction to Logotherapy*. He found that no particular background of the prisoners caused the differences. Frankl evaluated the major difference between the pessimists and optimists as being the hope for the future. Those who believed that their present sufferings would not cease and that the future only held additional sufferings gave up. Those who survived believed that the Nazis would ultimately be defeated and that the prisoners would be delivered to a better life. This hope gave them courage to endure. Hope for the future gave the prisoners a courage to endure the present.

God's people can stand many adverse circumstances of life. The reasons are neither personality types nor cultural background and conditioning.

The reason is that God's people believe that evil will ultimately be defeated, and they will be delivered to a better life in heaven.

HAROLD T. BRYSON

Romans 8:26-27 Prayer

On a rainy, stormy evening in 1945, I departed Algiers, Algeria, in a C47 for Bizerte, Tunisia. We had several passengers and some cargo aboard. About halfway to our destination, we encountered severe weather. We climbed as high as the plane would go but were not able to get above the storm. We encountered severe icing and lost all our radio equipment. We had no way to determine our exact location. We decided to attempt to return to Algiers. After flying for about thirty minutes, we broke out on top of the storm. It was the most beautiful sight I have ever seen. There was a full moon and a sky full of stars. In a few minutes, we saw a hole in the clouds and the lights of an airport runway were clearly visible below. We circled down through the opening and landed at Bizerte, our original destination.

I had been notified a few days earlier that I was the father of a healthy baby boy. I was very afraid during that storm that I would never see him. I am sure I prayed a very selfish prayer. I do not even remember what I prayed, but you can believe that I prayed. I was so busy trying to keep the plane in the air and get out of the storm that my words made little sense.

Paul reminded us in Romans that the Holy Spirit takes these babblings of ours and interprets their true intent to God. It is wonderful to know that the Holy Spirit makes intercession for us.

In Shakespeare's *Antony and Cleopatra,* Menecrates says:

> We, ignorant of ourselves,
> Beg often our own harms, which the wise powers
> Deny us for our good; so we find profit
> By losing of our prayers.[17]

Just as there are times when God hears our prayers and answers yes, there are times when he hears our prayers and answers no because in his goodness and mercy he knows that we are not praying as we ought.

JAMES A. YOUNG

Romans 8:28 Where Is God?

The pastor visited a family whose son had been killed in an automobile accident. The mother, deep in grief, railed out at the minister: "Where was your God when my boy was killed?"

Quietly, the minister answered the sufferer: "The same place he was when his own son was killed." So Moffatt's translation may be the clearest understanding of this verse: "We know also that those who love God, those who have been called in terms of purpose, have his aid, and interest in everything."

ROGER LOVETTE

Romans 8:28 Salvaging

A Jewish rabbi has written a book with an intriguing title: *When Bad Things Happen to Good People*. Harold S. Kushner is a Jewish rabbi in New England whose son, Aaron, died from progeria, the premature aging disease, two days past his fourteenth birthday. That book presents us with one of the most difficult problems we face in Christian living. Why is it that bad things happen to good people?

In trying to answer this question, we realize that there are no easy answers. The person who falls back on slick, stock answers fails to take into account the complexities of life. We like for things to be orderly, to always follow a cause/effect relationship. But as we struggle with these things, we become aware that we just can't always give a particular cause for a specific effect.

The Bible doesn't ever give us just one answer. As you search the Bible for the answers to that question, you soon realize that the Bible gives a number of answers. There are times when the reason may be punitive or probationary or educational or disciplinary or revelational or redemptive. But there are some times when accidents do happen and no particular cause can be found. A particular situation may not be necessarily any of those things.

In the end we turn to God, as Job did. He was able to confess that he had found God in personal experience, "I had heard of thee by the hearing of the ear,/but now my eye sees thee" (Job 42:5, RSV). Even though Job did not have his questions all answered, he did have God.

A favorite passage is Romans 8:28, "We know that in everything God works for good with those who love him, who are called according to his purpose" (RSV). Notice that it doesn't say that all things are good; a lot happens in this world that is not good. But also notice that God can work for good. As one of my friends expressed it, God is the great salvager. He can salvage any situation.

Bad things do happen to good people. But remember: when they do, God is still right there with you. And he can work in your life to give strength and hope right in the midst of it.

JAMES E. CARTER

Romans 8:28 Purpose

To an ignorant observer, the work of a surgeon might be an act of contradiction; in one moment he slashes into the body with his razor-sharp scalpel, and in the next moment he carefully binds the wounds and closes the arteries. It is important to remember that the purpose of both acts is one: the good of the person.[18]

J. DIXON FREE

Romans 8:28 Purpose

Those of us who like to watch western movies have seen it happen many times. The hero is shot in the shoulder by the villain; as he lies bleeding in the dust, the heroine who has stood by his side throughout the program brings a large hunting knife over to him, and he, "biting the bullet," lets her gouge that hunting knife into the bullet wound until she comes out with the piece of lead. We know without being told that she has had to do that destructive work in order for healing to take place in our hero. Though it hurts, we know it is important.

J. DIXON FREE

Romans 8:28 God's Hand

Alice Griffin, an American Baptist missionary to China, was expelled from that country in 1956 by the new Communist regime. Late in 1981, she was able to return for a visit—her first such opportunity in twenty-five years.

Her most moving experience was when a Chinese pastor she had known came to visit her. He told her that the church he had served was able to remain open until 1966. When the Red Guards came to the village, they closed the church and burned its contents. The pastor was arrested and sentenced to hard labor in prison.

He was released in 1979 and returned to the village. His body was broken from years of mistreatment. He discovered on his return that his wife was no longer living.

Word spread that the pastor was back, and the first night twelve people gathered for Bible study and prayer. Now one hundred people meet on Sundays and Thursdays for worship and study. This Chinese pastor trains them to witness and minister.

In Alice Griffin's words: "There he stood, a man with a broken body, with memories of a horrible life in prison, and of destruction and death.

Then he said to me, 'God's hand is working in all of this.'"

God works in all things.

DAVID MATTHEWS

Romans 8:28 Good Coming from Something Bad

A mariner was shipwrecked alone on a deserted island. Finally despairing of ever being rescued, he set about the task of seeking to make his exile as comfortable as possible. He cleared a place and built an encampment complete with a habitable shack. One day while he was off on the other side of the island on a hunting expedition, he saw a cloud of smoke rising above the trees. He immediately recognized that the smoke was coming from the area of his encampment. The man rushed through the jungle back to his campsite only to discover that his shack had caught fire and was engulfed in flames. In despair and defeat, he sat down to weep. But presently he heard sounds coming from the cove. Racing to the beach he saw a ship anchored offshore and a rescue party rowing into the lagoon. Once safe on the ship, the captain told the rescued mariner, "If it hadn't been for your signal fire, we would have never have known you were on that island." Out of what appeared to be a disaster, there had come good.

HARDY DENHAM

Romans 8:28 Things Work Together (Providence)

A woman in our church who worked with youth gave me a New Testament when I made it known that I felt God wanted me to preach.

On the white page in front where she had wished me well, she wrote a Scripture reference. It was Romans 8:28. I took that as a personal promise from God to me. There God promised to work all things together for good to "the called." And I had been called to preach, so this was a verse to me.

In time I came to understand that "the called" did not refer to preachers specifically but rather to all whom God called to believe and be saved. That made the verse even better because I could share it with all Christians and offer them divine comfort and hope.

Much time passed before I realized that I had unconsciously and unintentionally "bleeped out" a significant phrase in the verse. God will work things together for good to those who love him. To me the verse came to have a much greater meaning. I came to preach from this verse not only hope based on God's purpose but also the greatest of Christian obligations. Our major response to God should be to love him. And if we love God, everything that happens to us will work together for our good.

ELMER L. GRAY

Romans 8:30 Call

The summer after I graduated from high school I worked as a feed salesman. One of my customers was the Caddo Parish Penal Farm near Shreveport, Louisiana. Running a little later than usual one day, I arrived there shortly before lunch. After taking the order, the superintendent asked if I would stay and eat lunch with them. Acting coy, I mumbled something about having a lunch in the car. Really, I expected him to insist that I stay. But he did not press the invitation.

That evening at supper I told my family about the invitation to eat at the penal farm. My father told me that I had really erred. He told me that they ate well at the penal farm, especially the officers. After that I often made it a point to arrive at the penal farm near the lunch hour, but the invitation was never issued again.

God offers us an invitation to life. When that invitation is accepted, life in its fullest and most meaningful sense begins. God's mercy and grace are experienced.

But you have to accept the invitation. Unlike the penal farm superintendent, God continues to extend the invitation to us. Now we may act coy and try to get God to give us a special invitation with extra insistence. And to tell the truth, he does. In many ways, God continues to seek us and to ask us to come to him.

This is God's invitation to life. To accept the invitation is to accept life, to open the way to life giving and life enriching experiences. To reject the invitation is to close the door to life. Some things are self-inviting by their very nature. Accept God's invitation. Open the door to life.

JAMES E. CARTER

Romans 8:31 Hope

Noted painter Frederick Watts once painted a picture which he called *Hope*. In Watts's picture, a dejected female sits dejectedly atop the globe of the world. Her back is bent as though she is carrying some unbearable burden. The look of despair is on her face.

In one of her hands, Watts painted a lyre. All the strings of the instrument are broken except one.

As one looks at the picture, one wonders why Watts did not call his picture *Despair* instead of *Hope*. However, one quickly discovers the answer to his question in the one string on the lyre which is not broken. And as long as there is one string left, there is still hope that beautiful music can be produced from the instrument.

In one, brief, sweeping sentence in Romans 8:31, the apostle Paul gave us the answer to all of our despair and the basis of all our hope. He wrote: "If God be for us, who can be against us?"

J. B. FOWLER

Romans 8:31-39 Confidence in God

Friends once asked a man who was facing some grave problems in his life what was the outlook. The man readily replied that while the outlook might be dark, he could assure them that the uplook was wonderful. This is the attitude a person can possess only through the belief that Jesus Christ, the author and finisher of our faith, is going to be with her and sustain her in every experience. We who are believers are not to look ahead of us, behind us, about us, or even within us. We are instead to look to the face of Jesus Christ who assured us in a personal, tangible way of the love of God. In him we find peace in a troubled world, forgiveness for the burdens of sin, uplift from past difficulties and hope for the unknown future.

One of the gravest problems I observe in people today is their lack of self-confidence which is rooted in their lack of confidence in God. If we take God at his Word, we will believe we are persons of worth, we are redeemed by the power of Jesus Christ, and we are sustained through the presence of the Holy Spirit. When we do not feel confident before God, we are blown to and fro by every strong force that confronts us.

A writer once noted that a number of the world's great violinists felt they could not play well unless they had their favorite violins in their hands. In contrast, one of world's outstanding violinists is able to take any violin and make it sound superb. This is the way God works with us. He can play beautiful melodies out of every life placed in his hands. But we must open our lives to him so that our confidence in him becomes unshakable and our readiness to do his will become unfaltering. When you are in Christ, God hears you, God loves you, God answers you, God sustains you—forever!

ROBERT W. BAILEY

Romans 8:31-39 Nothing Can Separate

Eugene Laubach tells of the brilliant young English historian John Wilhelm Rowntree who discovered that his eyesight was failing when he was approaching the height of his career. Finally, his physician told him the dreaded truth: he would soon be totally blind.

Rowntree came out of that consultation into the street and stood in the sunlight for a few moments to collect himself. As he stood there, he wrote later, he "suddenly felt the love of God wrap him about as though an invisible presence enfolded him, and a joy filled him such as he had never known before."

To be going blind, to be faced with darkness before one's bright hopes for the future can be fulfilled, to stand at the edge of suffering and despair, and yet know the love of God, is to know the love of which Paul wrote. This is the love from which nothing can separate us.

DAVID MATTHEWS

Romans 8:32 God's Generosity

Suppose a person gave you a million dollars, and you wisely went to the bank and deposited your money, a portion of which you put in a checking account making it possible for you to be able to buy the things you need. Imagine that on one certain day you were walking through a shopping center with this man who gave you that large amount of money, and you chose a small item to purchase. You carried that item to the counter and reached into your pocket and found that you had left your checkbook and your wallet at home. You have no alternative but to turn to your benevolent friend and say, "Would you loan me ten dollars?"

Do you think that the man who gave you a million dollars would also loan you ten dollars? There is no question about it. The man whose heart is big enough to give you a million would not blink an eye at giving you ten. So it is that God's great gift of Jesus Christ to us indicates that the lesser gifts will just naturally follow from his great, loving, generous nature.

J. DIXON FREE

Romans 8:33-39 Suffering

L. D. Johnson received the crushing news of the death of his twenty-three-year-old daughter, Carole, in an icy highway accident. He waited sixteen years before he wrote about his own struggles with that tragic loss. He offered no easy answers. "The mystery of unmerited suffering remains; I know of no satisfactory explanation," he said. "But for the Christian there is an answer—not an explanation."

He found the answer in the incarnation, death, and resurrection of Jesus Christ. God had not abolished the hurts of human existence, he shared them and identified with them. In Christ God took the suffering and sin of humanity upon himself. He did not change the universe to make evil impossible and take away his gift of freedom of humanity. "Instead he partook of the cup of suffering himself and gave us the promise that nothing in all creation can separate us from his love."[19]

WILLIAM P. TUCK

Romans 8:35-39 Security in Christ

When my son was a toddler, he would come into the room where I was resting on Sunday afternoons and want to get on the bed with me. I would allow him to do so but with the understanding that I had to rest and he would have to also. That understanding would last about ten seconds. We would begin to play, what some call roughhouse. I would bounce him around on my legs like he was riding a bucking bronco. That's a dangerous thing to do with a small child on a bed. A fall to the floor could result in a broken bone, or worse. But Ross never fell. I always had a firm grip on one of his extremities.

Life can be a rough and tumbling experience, but God has a firm hold on the Christian. He may get knocked down, but he is secure in the grip of God.

HARDY DENHAM

Romans 8:38-39 God's Love

David Elkind, noted counselor and child psychologist, tells a story about observing his own son with three other boys in nursery school. The first boy said that his dad is a doctor who makes lots of money, and they have a swimming pool. The second little fellow informs the others that his dad is a lawyer who flies to Washington and talks with the president. The third boy, not to be outdone, relates that his father owns a company, and they own an airplane. Elkind's son came last. With great pride, little Elkind told the others, "My daddy is here!"

It is the love of God from which the people of God cannot be separated. It is the presence of God in Jesus Christ which makes real an otherwise abstract love.

W. WAYNE PRICE

Romans 8:38-39 Security

At PraiSing 1975 in Nashville when the new *Baptist Hymnal* was presented, many Christian entertainers were featured. A special hush fell over the auditorium when George Beverly Shea came to the microphone to sing. Before he sang, Bev Shea shared some of the experiences of his illustrious musical career. He explained how many people send songs to him in the mail for him to record. Some of these songs have potential. Most do not. The most amusing song he received was a song entitled, "God's Grip Don't Slip." This song is a rather quaint but accurate summary of the glorious truth with which Paul ended his eighth letter to the Romans: "For I am convinced that neither death, nor life, nor angels, nor principalities, nor things present, nor things to come, nor powers, nor height, nor depth, nor any other created thing, shall be able to separate us from the love of God, which is in Christ Jesus our Lord" (NASB). It is true: God's grip doesn't slip!

BRIAN L. HARBOUR

Romans 8:38-39 Death

John Donne wrote, "Death be not proud . . . /For those whom thou think'st thou dost overthrow,/Die not, poor death, nor yet canst thou kill me" (Holy Sonnets, No. 10). Paul asserted that nothing can cut a believer off from God—not even death.

From the human point of view, death appears to be destruction and tragedy. From God's point of view, death is departure to be with the Lord—it is triumph. Those who love God never say good-bye for the last time. Resurrection is the gift of God to those who believe.

ALTON H. MCEACHERN

Romans 9:1-3; 10:1 Concern for Others

Napoleon and his army confidently advanced into Russia in 1812. Even though he had been warned about Russian winters, Napoleon scoffed at the warning. By September 14 the French had reached Moscow.

The Russians launched a counterattack and the winter swiftly descended on the French. Napoleon was forced to order a retreat. The remnant of the once-proud French army finally crept back to France two months later. Napoleon had led more than 500,000 French soldiers into Russia, but less than 20,000 made it back to France. Most of these were suffering from typhus, frostbite, and starvation.

Napoleon didn't seem the least bit bothered that he had left the bulk of his army as frozen corpses in the Russian snow. He remarked to Metternich, "A man such as I is not much concerned over the lives of a million men."

Paul was concerned over the lives of his fellow Jews, and so much so that he would have given up his salvation if that would have resulted in their salvation.

HARDY DENHAM

Romans 9:2 Compassion, the Unending Pain

One estimate places a sixty billion dollar price tag on the annual health care expenditure for chronic pain sufferers.

Fortunately, relief is becoming more common. Through drugs, psychotherapy, surgery, exercise, biofeedback, external electrical stimulation, nerve block therapy, medical hypnosis, acupuncture, and other methods used at pain clinics and centers, help is being given to many people who previously found no relief.

As demonstrated in Paul's compassion for fellow Jews, there is one pain that believers must not seek to remove. It is the continuing burden carried for those without Christ. It is the chronic pain of compassion. Relief comes only when the unsaved receive Christ.

ERNEST D. STANDERFER

Romans 9:11 Election

The doctrine of election is a difficult concept to understand. Perhaps nothing helped me more about the doctrine of election than an incident in my family. My wife and I have two sons who are only one year apart in age. When they were five and six years of age, my wife needed some bread from the grocery store. Since both boys looked constantly for excuses to ride their bicycles to the local grocery store, I decided to send one of the boys. But which one would I choose? Both were qualified. For some unexplainable reason I selected the younger one. He was selected to get bread which the entire family would enjoy.

On the way to the grocery store, the boy became interested in other friends as they played football. He decided to delay his trip for a while. Meanwhile the rest of the family waited for the bread. I looked for the boy and discovered where he was and what he was doing. Immediately, I turned to the other son. He got the bread.

The incident might help the doctrine of election. God chose Israel to be a mission to the nation. Israel was to bring the "bread of life" to the rest of the world. She went after other affections, and she forsook God and his purpose. Naturally God turned to another group, redeemed Gentiles, to bring the message to the nations.

HAROLD T. BRYSON

Romans 9:22 Vessels Fitted to Destruction

As the potter has power over the clay, vessels of wrath are fitted to destruction as God's power is eventually known.

History reminds us of this truth over and over. More than forty years ago, Adolf Hitler and his henchmen walked amid the spectacular mountains and lakes of Bavaria's Obersalzberg. Barracks for SS guards, houses for close associates, a theater, and a hotel provided a plush resort setting to receive foreign diplomats. Hitler's "Eagle's Nest," a grey brick building perched on the 6,017-foot-high tip of Hoher Boell, created the illusion that from that vantage point he felt he could rule the world.

Today, 215,000 tourists a year brave the bus ride up a narrow road to see the place where the infamous dictator once ruled. No traces are left. Tourists can visit the remains of Hitler's bunker, 578 feet under Obersalzberg, but no plaques mark the Berghof or the villas of Hitler's deputies, Martin Bormann and Hermann Goering.

Only memories, the beautiful view, and a lesson for the ages are left: little people may strut across the stage of history for a little while, but God's power will be evident in time as these vessels are fitted to destruction.

JACK GULLEDGE

Romans 10:1; 10:13-17 Concern for Others

The inscription on Mohandas K. Gandhi's Black Stone in New Delhi, India, reads as follows: "My prayer for my country is that India would someday be strong enough to give herself for the world: a man for his family, a family for a village, a village for a district, a district for the country, the country for the world."

At the time of the writing of Romans, Paul, no doubt, maintained a hope that Israel might mediate God's love for the redemption of the world. But

Israel's rejection of Jesus Christ meant that Paul's most basic hope had to rest simply in Israel's need to be saved. It was a passionate hope, based upon his love for his people.

W. WAYNE PRICE

Romans 10:5-15 Knowing Where to Be

My father tells of a man in southwest Virginia who used to be an outstanding fox trapper. Dozens of those mountaineers would seek to trap these animals to save their small livestock and to sell the valuable furs. But it seemed that this one man would trap more foxes in a week than the rest of the men in the county put together would trap in a month. When about all the foxes had been trapped, the man finally told his secret for success. He said he would walk through the woods thinking like a fox. He would pretend he was looking for something to eat and suddenly heard some dogs chasing him. He would stand on a log and look around and decide which way to jump off the log. And right at the very point he felt a fox would jump off that log, he placed his trap. Invariably, he would go back and have a fox in it! He was successful because he anticipated how certain circumstances would appear and appeal to a fox.

We may hoard, scrape, and accumulate, but we do not come to live as God intended until we see that we are stewards of what he has entrusted to us for a season. We are to use our possessions and lives as a means of service in the Father's name. Neither our lives nor our goods are given to us in abstract. God clothes and equips us to be his stewards on mission! It is both a privilege and responsibility to live a life created by God and have opportunities bestowed on us by him. Our temporary ownership of things of this world is intended for us to know joy and practice justice. It is wrong for us to be selfish and neglect the poor. It is wrong for us to live beyond our means and fuel the inflationary fires. It is wrong for us to be selfish and fail to care for our family's needs. It is wrong for us to keep everything for the family and fail to use our resources to share God's good news in Christ around the world. It is wrong for us to be so self-centered that we neglect to be in the right place with the right means to proclaim salvation to those searching for a Savior. We will experience the joy of our salvation when we determine to do our best to use our best in the right place for the sake of Christ and a lost world.

ROBERT W. BAILEY

Romans 10:8,16-21 Bible

The Word of God is certainly near the people of America. In 1981 $170 million was spent for Bibles. One recent edition of *Books in Print* requires fifty-five pages to list all its Bible-related entries while fifteen are concerned with food. Church historian Martin Marty notes the Bible in America has joined the Declaration of Independence and the Constitution as an American "icon." Despite the Bible's availability, there is much biblical illiteracy. A 1979 Gallup Poll survey found that only 49 percent of Protestants and 44 percent of Roman Catholics could name as many as four of the Ten Commandments.[20] The problem remains the same today as always—"They have not all obeyed the gospel; . . . 'All day long I have held out my hands to a disobedient and contrary people'" (vv. 16,21, RSV).

BILL D. WHITTAKER

Romans 10:9 Jesus Is Lord

Herman was seventy-six years old when I met him. A friend of his, a deacon in our church, took me by to witness to Herman. Charlie had witnessed to him on many occasions. As I shared the plan of salvation with Herman, I asked him if he were willing to call upon the name of the Lord and ask him to save him. Herman replied in the affirmative. We got down on our knees in front of his couch, and Herman repeated a prayer of salvation after me. I then asked him if he were a Christian.

He replied, "No, I'm not." I had him to repeat a prayer of salvation two more times. Each time he would reply, "I still don't think I'm a Christian."

Charlie then said, "Herman, tell me that Jesus is your Lord."

Herman looked at Charlie and said, "Jesus is my Lord."

Charlie said, "Herman, tell your wife that Jesus is your Lord."

Herman said, "Betty, Jesus is my Lord."

Charlie admonished him, "Herman, tell my wife that Jesus is your Lord."

Herman said, "Hazel, Jesus is my Lord."

Charlie replied, "Herman, tell my pastor that Jesus is your Lord."

Herman looked at me and tried to get out the words and couldn't. Tears came to his eyes, he choked up, and he shook his head. I knew that Jesus had become his Lord. We need to confess that Jesus is our Lord.

BILL BRUSTER

Romans 10:13 Salvation for Everyone

The desert fathers told a parable of God's inexhaustible mercy. According to the ancient tale, Satan stood beside Christ just outside the gates of heaven. A steady stream of the dregs of humanity approached the gates and were waved through by the nail-imprinted hand of Christ. Satan's anger increased until in a rage he exploded: "Drunkards, thieves, traitors, murderers, and you open your kingdom to them. Their deeds are far darker than mine. Why have you not invited me through the portals?"

Jesus' quiet response, "Because you never asked." Such is the depth of mercy revealed at Calvary.

RAYMOND H. BAILEY

Romans 10:13 Salvation

Most basketball fans immediately recognize the name Dr. J., for he is one of the greatest players ever to play the game. Dr. J., Julius Irving, is one of the two active players named to the all-time, all-star team. Dr. J. has had many thrills on the basketball court, but the most important time in his life did not involve athletics. The highlight of his life happened when he was twenty-nine years of age, and it grew out of a crisis in his life.

An injury to his leg seemed to jeopardize his career. His leg was not responding to the treatment, and he was getting discouraged. In that time of despair, Julius went to a family reunion with three hundred members of the Irving family. In his discussion with those relatives, Julius discovered the strong Christian influence which was a part of the heritage of his life. He learned of one uncle who prayed for him two generations before he was ever born and prayed that when he was born, God would bless him.

Realizing he had not built anything of eternal value on that spiritual heritage, Dr. J. began to examine his own life. He recognized his spiritual emptiness. He realized that he needed a Savior. So one night, in the quietness of his own home, Dr. J. claimed the promise of Romans 10:13: "Whoever will call upon the name of the Lord will be saved" (NASB). According to Julius Irving, it was that moment which was the highlight of his life, for it has given him a purpose to live for and a power to live by.

BRIAN L. HARBOUR

Romans 10:13 Invitation to Call to the Lord

Two American women who were musicians were on a concert tour of Korea.

They made an appointment to go to a beauty parlor and prayed that on the way that they would have an opportunity to witness while they were there.

As the beauticians worked on the American women, a Korean businesswoman who was single and in her mid-30s spoke to one of the Americans.

"You married?" she asked.

"No," replied the American.

"You happy?"

"Yes, but my happiness is not because I am unmarried. It is because of my relationship with Jesus."

A discussion developed that attracted the attention of others around. The American moved over under the noisy dryer but continued trying to talk.

She hollered the plan of salvation above the noise of the dryer. Everyone in the beauty parlor who understood English heard how to be saved. In the meantime, the other American woman had been praying. By the time the American came out from under the dryer, the Korean was ready to receive Christ. They found a quiet place for prayer. And the Korean woman accepted God's invitation to trust Jesus Christ and be saved.[21]

ELMER L. GRAY

Romans 10:14-15 Missions

Doris Smith served for over twenty years as a missionary in Venezuela. On March 10, 1983, she won the victory over a year-long fight with malignancy. Her funeral was conducted on the following Saturday. During the service, "How Great Thou Art" was sung with the second verse in Spanish. I thought of the many people in South America with whom Doris, her husband, Don, and their five children had shared the greatness of God. Following the benediction the family filed out behind the casket as the organ played, "My house is full, my fields are empty . . . who will go and work the fields today?" The Lord seemed to say—"Who will take Doris' place?" How are they to hear unless someone goes to tell them?

BILL D. WHITTAKER

Romans 11:8 Ears that Do not Hear

Several people applied for a job with a steamship company. They filled the outer office with a buzz of conversation; they paid no attention to the dots and dashes which began coming over a loudspeaker. Another man entered the office and sat down quietly by himself. Suddenly he snapped to attention, walked into the private office, and in a few minutes came out smiling.

Someone asked him why he was so happy. "Because I got the job," he replied. He explained, "If you had been listening to the message from the loudspeaker, you could have gotten the job."

"What message?" they asked.

"The coded message that said: 'The man I need must always be on the alert. The first man who gets this message and comes directly into my private office will be placed on one of my ships as operator.' "[22]

We, Paul reminded us, like ancient Israel get so noisy and inattentive that we fail to be alert to hear God's message to our hearts. We unfortunately have "the spirit of slumber, eyes that they should not see, and ears that they should not hear."

JACK GULLEDGE

Romans 11:25-27 Salvation of Jews

One American out of thirty is Jewish. That means that the United States has almost eight million Jews living in it. That is about half of the Jews in the world. More Jews live in this nation than in Israel. To a great extent these Jews have concentrated in five states—New York, California, Florida, New Jersey, and Pennsylvania.

Paul continued through his ministry to care for his own people, the Jews. He urged the Christians at Rome not to despise Jews but to appreciate them for what they had received from them in the way of knowledge about God. Paul taught that, when God had brought the full number of Gentiles into his kingdom, he would reach out to save all of Israel.

Is it simply an accident of history that such a large number of Jews live in the United States where so many Christians live? What would Paul say to American Christians about the Jews who live among them? He reminded the Christians in Rome that salvation for Jews is the same as salvation for Gentiles. Humanity's one Deliverer is Jesus Christ. What an opportunity American Christians have to witness to and to work with Jews!

ELMER L. GRAY

Romans 11:33-36 Doxology

Doxologies sometimes appear in what may seem unlikely places. The reader of Romans might not have expected a hymn of praise from Paul at this point.

It is told that during the Civil War prisoners from the Union Army were being held in a certain prison in the South. Each day some would die and new prisoners would arrive. It was a very depressing, hopeless place.

One day from the suffering in the cold cells, a lone voice sang out: "Praise God, from whom all blessings flow." A dozen joined on the second line. Nearly all sang the final words, "Praise Father, Son, and Holy Ghost." It was not the first time or the last that strange situations have broken open with praise.

David Matthews

Romans 12:1 Concern

When the apostle Paul used the phrase, "I beseech you" he was using a loving, tender expression which means "to call up by the side of." This phrase carries with it a picture of a brother who comes up beside another brother and, putting his arm around him, comforts, strengthens, and pleads with him to do that which is right.

The word for brother here denotes blood kin. Now certainly Paul was not blood kin to the members of the church at Rome except for the fact that they all were redeemed and washed in the same blood—the blood of the Lamb—Jesus Christ. They were brothers in Christ.

J. Dixon Free

Romans 12:1 Commitment

A chicken and a pig passed a beggar sitting on the sidewalk. They discussed some way to help him. The chicken proposed they give him a breakfast of ham and eggs. The pig replied, "From you that's just a gift, but from me that is total commitment!"

BILL D. WHITTAKER

Romans 12:1-2 Integrity

Several years ago when a church where I was pastor was looking for an assistant minister, we received the following letter of reference from a young man's former college professor. "There is something wonderfully clean about the young man, and the reference there is to his mind as well as to his physical being. He is unfailingly a gentleman. . . . He is loyal to the very highest ideals, and he has both the intelligence and the character to render estimable service to these ideals. I believe that if there is one word that summarizes his many splendid qualities, it is *integrity*, and I like to think of the relationship of that word to *integer*. He is a 'whole number,' solid and sound and unblemished." Obviously, we called him. What the Christian says is intimately involved with how he or she lives. Words and deeds are linked together.

WILLIAM P. TUCK

Romans 12:1-2 Transformed not Conformed

One of the great black preachers of the twentieth century was Howard Thurman. He was author of a score of books, the first black chaplain of

Boston University in the forties, and listed as one of America's greatest preachers. For years he served on the staff of Howard University in Washington, D.C. Dr. Thurman's life was beset with many struggles. He could have found many reasons to have conformed to the image that the world placed on black people ninety years ago, yet he refused to accept those limitations.

He grew up on the "wrong side of the tracks" in Jacksonville, Florida. In one of the last interviews that he gave before his death, someone asked him what had kept him going when life was so hard and difficult. Thurman began to talk about his grandmother who had once been a slave. He said when his grandmother knew that the water was getting low in the well of his life, she would tell him a story. It would always be the same story, and it was a tale that came out of her own past.

She would tell her grandson that when she was a young woman she was a slave on a plantation. Once a year and sometimes more frequently, the minister, who was himself a slave on a neighboring plantation, was permitted to hold religious services for the slaves. Always, no matter what his subject was, the preacher ended his sermon the same way. She said that he would stand and look down on them. Then he would say, "You are not slaves, you are not niggers—you are God's children."

Thurman said when his grandmother would tell him that story she would always get a faraway look in her eyes, and her spine would stiffen slightly. Thurman said even as a boy he felt the contagion of knowing the Creator of existence had created him. With that sort of backing, Thurman said, he would absorb all the violences of life. When we realize we are children of God, we find ourselves transformed by the incredible grace of God.

ROGER LOVETTE

Romans 12:2 Thermometers or Thermostats

Phillip's translation helps us to understand Paul's intention of this verse: "Don't let the world around you squeeze you into its own mould, but let God re-make you so that your whole attitude of mind is changed. Thus you will prove in practice that the will of God's good, acceptable to him and perfect." One minister caught the true intent of these words in a sermon he called "Thermometers or Thermostats."

He held up two simple household items, a thermometer and a thermostat. He saw these as representatives of all of our lives. He said a thermometer is only a recorder of temperature. The thermometer is an instrument that reflects how hot or how cold it is on a given day. It is useful in letting us know about the weather, but that is as far as it goes.

Next, he held up a thermostat. The thermostat not only reflects the temperature but it goes further. By simply turning the dial, the temperature can be changed. This instrument has been designed to do something about the temperature. As Paul spoke to his Roman audience, he knew that they were either reflectors of the culture around them or they could become those rare individuals that try to do something positive about the world they live in.

ROGER LOVETTE

Romans 12:2 Transformation

All of us have our "most embarrassing moment" in the pulpit or in some life situation. Mine came one Sunday while preaching on this passage. I was attempting to explain what Paul meant by "being transformed."

The Greek word for transformation is the same word as the English word *metamorphosis*. It is a combination of two Greek words, *meta* meaning change and *morpha* meaning nature. Webster illustrates the meaning with two comparisons, the changing of a tadpole into a frog and the changing of a cocoon into a silkworm. I was waxing eloquent and was at the climax of my illustration when I said, "It is the process of changing a tadpole into a frog or a raccoon into a silkworm." That would be quite a transformation. I laughed with the congregation when I realized what I had said, but I expect those folk will remember my illustration better than they would have without the mistake.

The transforming power of God that changes a tadpole into a frog operates in our lives if we allow it to do so. The purpose of this transformation is to equip us to understand the will and purpose of God for our lives.

James A. Young

Romans 12:3 Identity

My wife has a nephew whose name is James Harrell Hunter. My father-in-law's name is also James Harrell Hunter. His grandfather was named James Harrell Hunter also.

When James was about three years old, his grandfather was on his knees doing some weeding in the garden one day. Little James walked right up to him and put his face right in the grandfather's face with their noses almost touching and said, "G-daddy, what is your name?"

Mr. Hunter rocked back on his knees and replied, "My name is James Harrell Hunter the second. You are James Harrell Hunter the third." James then threw down his hoe, got red in the face, and said, "G-daddy, my not be third!"

That pretty well expresses our attitude, doesn't it? We don't want to be third. Whether in name, in rank, or in standing, we don't want to be third. We want to be first.

We express this in different ways. Sometimes we talk about "looking out for number one." Watch and see how people will find some way to move up in a line. Everybody wants to play first chair in the band. Not too many people are anxious to play third cornet, third chair. Athletes want to be on the starting team, and they have been known to quit the team when they could no longer start. Nobody wants to be third!

Christian faith encourages us to think of others as well as ourselves. We are to have a concern, an interest, a compassion for others and their problems.

I have heard of Sunday School classes and other organizations with the name J.O.Y. It means "Jesus first, Others second, Yourself last." That is a commendable line up.

We don't like to be third, or anything but first for that matter, but it sometimes helps when we are willing to put another and his welfare first. Remember what Paul told the Roman Christians, "Do not think of yourself more highly than you should. Instead, be modest in your thinking, and judge yourself according to the amount of faith that God has given you" (Rom. 12:3, GNB).

JAMES E. CARTER

Romans 12:3 Self-Esteem

The warning "not to think of himself more highly than he ought" also involves the danger of thinking less of self than one ought. In a survey among women, psychologist James Dobson found low self-esteem to be the leading problem.

BILL D. WHITTAKER

Romans 12:4 Church

John Bishop, in his book *Seeing Jesus Today: A Portrait of Jesus the Man,* tells of the construction of a church building in a large American city. The building was nearing completion. Workmen were installing the lights. The pews were being fastened into place. On a large high wall above the communion table there was a large picture of Christ as the Good Shepherd in the process of being painted. The artist had only outlined the head and shoulders of the Master. A stranger stepped inside the church building and looked around curiously. He asked one of the workmen when the picture would be finished.

"That picture?" the workman asked, pointing to the wall. "It is finished."

"Finished," said the startled visitor, "why, most of it is still missing. The eyes, mouth, arms, hands, legs and feet—the whole body is missing."

"You won't see that on a wall," the workman replied. "The body of

Christ is the congregation who will be worshipping in this building. The body of Christ is the church."[23]

HAROLD T. BRYSON

Romans 12:3-8 Church; Body of Christ; Shared Ministry

The effectiveness of the church often depends upon the degree to which every person submits to the purposes of God. An apocryphal Leonard Bernstein story makes the point. Bernstein was to conduct the orchestra in a performance of a concerto which was to be done with pianist Glenn Gould. Before the performance, Bernstein is reported to have turned to the audience and said, "Mr. Gould and I could not agree upon an interpretation of this piece, so we have decided to play it each in our own way." How like the church. We are so often guilty of sublimating the plan of God to individual interests.

In a more generous and expansive spirit, Norman Cousins left his post of thirty-five years as editor of the *Saturday Review* to teach humanities to UCLA medical students. This then-sixty-three-year-old enthusiast commented, "What a wonderful way to pick up knowledge. There's only one of you and perhaps seventy-five of them."

Even more exemplary was Gregory I, Roman Catholic pope from AD 590, founder of seven monasteries. When he accepted the office after a period of severe struggle, he accepted to become "a servant of the servants of God." Such is the place of the individual within the body of Christ.

W. WAYNE PRICE

Romans 12:4-8 Gifts

As the music of Handel's *Hallelujah Chorus* built to its dramatic ending, no one in the sanctuary remained unmoved by the music and its deep emotion and meaning.

The tour group stood in awe while viewing *The Last Supper* of Michelangelo. God's magnificent gifts of music and art bring inexpressible joy to many lives—especially to those enriched by having these gifts and sharing them with others.

Lesser-recognized gifts include listening with sensitivity to persons in need, visiting the sick and lonely, or giving understanding to troubled individuals. Even ordinary things, not usually considered as talents, assume new significance when viewed as gifts—cleaning buildings for the comfort and benefit of others, repairing cars for the safety of others, or organizing meetings for the growth of others.

GAGE MCMAHON

Romans 12:4-8 Gifts

Several years ago my wife, Emily, and I were attending a Sunday School class party. We were all seated in chairs in a circle. The leader said to me, "Bill, take Emily's place."

"I can't," I responded. Oh, I knew what he meant. But I wanted to make a point.

I could not really take Emily's place. She has her own distinctive gifts and abilities. I contribute mine, and she shares her own. We cannot take each other's place in the church, but each of us shares in his or her own ministry. So it is with all of us. Each of us brings to the church's ministry the gifts he or she possesses and shares them in service for Christ. In the eyes of Christ, all gifts are sufficient. We do not take each other's place, but we labor together in a variety of ways. Each serves not for reward or recognition, hopefully, but for the joy of sharing one's own gift in the ministry of Christ.

WILLIAM P. TUCK

Romans 12:9 Hate What Is Evil

A woman was interviewing prospective carriage drivers. She asked, "If you were driving my carriage down a road with a cliff and a one-thousand foot drop on one side, how close could you drive to the edge without allowing the carriage to fall over?"

One man answered that he could drive just six inches from the cliff safely; another answered three inches; and one said just one inch from the cliff. A fourth prospect for the job answered, "If I were driving your carriage, I would stay as far from the edge of that cliff as I could." He was the man who got the job.

HARDY DENHAM

Romans 12:9-13 Brotherly Love

Luther Joe Thompson has said a community of love has power to heal. Thompson, former pastor of First Baptist Church, Richmond, Virginia, stated this in his book *Love Is Alive*.

He reported that a psychiatrist once said to him, "If you church people would really be church in the Christian sense, you could do what all the psychiatrists on earth could not do." And the psychiatrist talked enthusiastically to the preacher about the potential that a loving church has for healing people of such hurts as cynicism, brokenness, depression, confusion, and rebellion.

Thompson wrote, "To belong to God is to belong to each other. . . . In the community of faith we come to know a Savior's love; we discover the wonder of forgiveness; we learn what it means to love and to be loved; we learn how to reach out to help, to heal, and to set free."[24]

Love is one of the most universal needs in the world. Many people live and die without learning how to love and to accept love. With great concern

Paul urged Christians to love each other and to show their love in kind acts of helpfulness.

ELMER L. GRAY

Romans 12:11 Responsibility

The Revised Standard Version of the Bible translates the words of the King James Version of the Bible "fervent in Spirit" with the words "be aglow with the Spirit"; Barclay, "Keep your spirit at boiling point"; Phillips, "keep the fires of the spirit burning"; and Williams, "always on fire with the Spirit."

Edward Gibbon, describing the tenth-century Greek scholars in Constantinople, wrote:

> They held in their lifeless hands the riches of their fathers, without inheriting the spirit which had created and improved that sacred patrimony: they read, they praised, they compiled, but their languid souls seemed alike incapable of thought and action. In the revolution of ten centuries, not a single discovery was made to exalt the dignity or promote the happiness of mankind.[25]

Gibbon's words warn us of the danger that faces people who lose their spiritual glow. It does not happen in a single act of disobedience; it is more subtle. It occurs day by day as we fail to give attention to our spiritual lives. John Newport of Southwestern Baptist Theological Seminary reminded us often that we are never more than one generation away from paganism. Gibbon continued his warning by writing, "The leaders of the Greek church were humbly content to admire and copy the oracles of antiquity, nor did the schools or pulpit produce any rivals of the fame of Athanasius and Chrysostom."

JAMES A. YOUNG

Romans 12:11 Zeal

Spiritual zeal can wane. E. Stanley Jones told once of a Chinese scholar who was commissioned to translate Augustine's massive volume *City of God*. After some time he sent this message to the mission board. "I would like another assignment. I am tired of working on the *City of God*."

DAVID MATTHEWS

Romans 12:12 A Reason to Rejoice

It has been long recognized that a happy spirit or outlook helps a person function better. One university professor has suggested that our attitudes and job productivity would improve if we laughed about forty-three times a day. He even conducts laughter therapy workshops for business people.

A good laugh does help, but laughing can be superficial. We need more than a good laugh. We need a reason to rejoice and enjoy life.

Paul pointed to the Christian reason for rejoicing—the hope we have in Christ. This is a hope that transcends earthly problems and unwelcome circumstances.

ERNEST D. STANDERFER

Romans 12:12 Ceaseless Prayer

Mark Twain's character, Huck Finn, is amusing to us on the surface. Deep down Huck expresses a lot of our own inner feelings. Huck once commented that Miss Watson took him in the closet and prayed, but nothing ever came of the prayer. Miss Watson told him to pray every day, and he would get whatever he asked for. But Huck found that his prayers did not work. He tried without success. One time he got a fishing line, and he needed some hooks. He prayed three or four times for hooks but never got any. In his disappointed frustration, Huck sat down in the woods one day and thought about the supposed effectiveness of prayer. He concluded that if prayer got you what you wanted, then Deacon Winn would get back the money he lost farming that year, the old widow would get back her silver snuffbox that had been stolen, and Miss Watson would gain some weight for her fragile frame. But since none of these persons got what they wanted and he did not get what he wanted, Huck said to himself that there was nothing to prayer.

Twain makes us smile at Huck Finn while he tells us the reason most people quit praying—it just does not seem to work for them! Unfortunately too many persons—even church members—view prayer as something to use for their desires as long as it works for them! But this is never what God intended prayer to be. He desires to have communion with his people. He wants us to be open and receptive to him and his leading. Prayer was never intended to be our means of manipulating a divine genie. Prayer was offered us so that we might come in tune with God, receive his power, and be able to offer our spiritual energy to others.

Paul described the life-style of the faithful Christian as one who engages in ceaseless prayer. He was speaking both of the attitude of the one praying and the choice of words we use in praying. We are, as Jesus taught, to pray for what we need, but the major emphasis of our praying is to give thanks to our great God and recommit ourselves to his disposal. We grow in prayer and in the Christian life only as we are constant in our prayer.

ROBERT W. BAILEY

Romans 12:14 Hostility

A news report on a meeting of an American Heart Association Seminar reported that two well-documented studies showed that people with angry, hostile outlooks have a high risk of dying of heart attack. One study showed that persons with high hostility ratings had five times the risk of dying from any cause as those who had low hostility rating. Such people tend to live in fear and suspicion of others. Blessing those who persecute and curse you may bring about physical as well as spiritual well-being. Christ's way has immediate as well as future benefits.

RAYMOND H. BAILEY

Romans 12:14-21 Dealing with Enemies

A man was found unconscious on a city street. He was taken to a hospital for treatment. When he regained consciousness, the man began to verbally abuse all who tried to help him. He became so obnoxious that the attendants began to avoid him—all except one nurse. She brought his medication, bathed him, changed his bed linens, and continued to minister to his needs in spite of the foul and offensive things he said to her. Finally, the day came for the man to be discharged. The nurse stopped by his bed to tell him good-bye. Somewhat repentant the man asked, "I want to know something. I've acted awful toward you, cursing you, insulting you. Yet, you did not do like the others and leave me alone. Why?"

The nurse responded, "God loves you, and I felt that maybe he wanted to love you through me."

HARDY DENHAM

Romans 12:15 Shared Grief

There is a Chinese tale about a woman whose only son died. In great grief she went to a holy man and asked, "What prayers or what magical incantations do you have to bring my son back to life?"

Instead of sending her away or reasoning with her, he said, "Fetch me a mustard seed from a home that has never known sorrow. We will use it to drive the sorrow out of your life."

The woman set off at once in search of the mustard seed. She came first to a splendid mansion, knocked at the door, and said, "I am looking for a home that has never known sorrow. Is this such a place?"

They told her, "You've certainly come to the wrong place," and described all the tragic things that had recently befallen them. The woman said to herself, "Who is better able to help these poor, unfortunate people than I who had misfortune of my own?" So she stayed to comfort them, then went on in her search for a home that had never known sorrow.

But wherever she went, in hovels or palaces, she found one experience after another of sadness and misfortune. Ultimately, she became so involved in ministering to the grief of others that she forgot about the magical mustard seed. Her quest had given her the answer to her sorrow.

David Matthews

Romans 12:16 Humility

What Christian is not tempted to relax in the pilgrimage of faith, especially when a few consecutive victories make one confident of personal achievement? I am often helped by an observation of a respected member of Alcoholics Anonymous. I asked him how a mutual friend seemed to be progressing in his struggle with the disease. He responded that the man was doing remarkably well. Then he added, "I just don't want him to graduate." In every difficult climb, the enemy is overconfidence. When the climber begins to feel too comfortable, a slip may be a part of the next step.

W. Wayne Price

Romans 12:18 Living Peaceably

The news media carried the story in March, 1982, about a little town in the northwest that ended up with virtually no leaders. Squabbling led to the resignation of the mayor, city recorder, city attorney, city clerk, public works director, several city council members, and other officials. The police chief's resignation was to take effect when a replacement could be appointed. Obviously there will be no progress until the squabbling stops and citizens fulfill their responsibilities.

Sometimes churches and individuals fall into the squabbling habit. Confusion and stagnation result. The Bible admonished us to do all that is possible to live peaceably with all people.

ERNEST D. STANDERFER

Romans 13:1 Authority

The question of civil obedience and civil disobedience has been one of the most difficult of our time. It cannot be decided apart from ultimate authority. Bishop James A. Pike, tried for heresy by the Episcopal Church, may have thrown much light on the matter when he said that he has no authority who does not himself stand under authority.

W. WAYNE PRICE

Romans 13:1-7 Law Enforcers

A police chief in a large city was criticized for not enforcing all the laws with the same degree of effort. He and his men enforced some laws rigidly and actually ignored others.

The chief answered honestly. He admitted that the police didn't even know all of the laws on the books. They could not possibly give equal attention to all of them. Instead they majored on those that people expected them to enforce and on those that community leaders asked them to give attention to.

Government in a democracy is much more complicated than the monarchy or dictatorship that Paul lived in. In Paul's day, the ruler was both lawmaker and law enforcer. Paul advised Christians to obey persons in power. In our times that would mean to obey the law.

In these times Christians must become concerned about the whole legal process. They need to influence the lawmaking bodies, support and encourage officers of the law, and help to speed up the judging procedures of trying and sentencing lawbreakers. This is a day when public opinion can influence governmental processes. Therefore, being a Christian citizen today is more than obeying the law; it is helping to shape and enforce good laws.

ELMER L. GRAY

Romans 13:1-7 Authority

Before the concert, musicians gathered on stage. As each began to play his or her instrument, chaos resulted. From offstage, one person came to the podium. Quickly, the noise of undisciplined sound ceased as the musicians prepared to begin the concert. They recognized the need for only one person—the conductor—to have the leadership role during the concert.

To have order, whether in symphony concerts, schools, churches, cities, or nations, the authority of those who lead needs to be respected. Ultimately, all authority comes from God.

GAGE MCMAHON

Romans 13:6-7 Paying Taxes

When a leading newsmagazine features an article on how taxpayers are cheating on the government, the problem must be serious. On March 28, 1983, *Time* magazine reported that tax evasion was approaching an epidemic stage, and many honest people were being hurt by it. One interesting item in the report related cheating on taxes to social climbing.

Many believe it's a sign of stupidity to pay all taxes. Ways discovered to avoid such payments provide something to brag about on social occasions.

Speaking before a Bible study group, one man confessed that he had never been caught on his income tax report. He quickly explained that he meant to say he had never been checked.

The Scripture is clear. Christians, as citizens, have taxpaying responsibilities. Whether the world considers it stupid or not in vogue matters not; the biblical claim stands.

ERNEST D. STANDERFER

Romans 13:11-14 Time to Wake Up

A number of years ago Dr. Carl Bates, then pastor of First Baptist Church in Charlotte, North Carolina, wrote an account that has stuck with me. He reported from his research that the cattle tick is a little bloodsucking insect with an amazing life history. When it comes from the egg, the tick is not fully developed. It does not have legs, nor can it reproduce. Even in that state it can attack cold-blooded animals, such as frogs and lizards. After it grows and sheds its skin several times, it acquires the rest of its body, a mate, and then can attack and take blood from warm-blooded animals. The female has no eyes. She is directed to the tip of a twig on a bush by her skin which is photosensitive. She stays on the edge of that bush through night and day, cold weather and hot—waiting for the moment she can fulfill her purpose in life.

In a zoo these female cattle ticks have been observed to stay on the end of twigs for eighteen years! Eighteen years of waiting for just the right moment! Eighteen years of doing nothing but waiting. That tick waits for the scent of sweat in all animals. And when a person or a dog walks by that twig, for the first time in her life that tick's reason for living has come! She leaps on to that animal, buries herself in the flesh, and does what she is supposed to do.

Since Dr. Bates had been at First Charlotte for eighteen years at that point, he asked his people when they were going to get off their twig and do what they were meant to do! Paul echoed this need for urgency when he told the Romans it was time for them to wake from sleep, throw off the works of darkness, and be busy about the work Christ had for them.

ROBERT W. BAILEY

Romans 13:11 Time

We spent a portion of our summer vacation one year on South Padre Island in Texas. That was our first encounter with that part of Texas, and we thoroughly enjoyed it.

Being that close to Mexico, we thought we ought to make at least one excursion south of the border. So the three families from our church who were at the same place at the same time got themselves somewhat organized and took off for Matamoros. Stopping at the border in Brownsville, we decided to leave our cars on the USA side of the border and take a bus across the river and into the city of Matamoros. We were assured by the uniformed man at the border station that the bus would stop on the corner by the bridge every fifteen minutes. For a mere thirty cents each we could board the bus, cross the border, and ride to the marketplace. That sounded feasible to us. So to the corner we went to wait for the bus that came every fifteen minutes.

We waited an hour and twenty minutes! That was our first wave of cultural shock. With the North American's dependence on calendars and clocks, we were ready for the bus that comes every fifteen minutes—only it took an hour and twenty minutes. No amount of fretting, fussing, or fuming seemed to hurry it a bit. Looking down the street, walking to the next corner, going to the bridge, crossing the street for a cold drink all yielded no results. We were powerless. It was all out of our hands.

How much of life has been spent waiting for something that you could neither command nor control?

Maybe it was the big break you were waiting for.

Maybe it was the years of schooling and preparation preparing yourself for the opportunity that perhaps would come.

Maybe it was the promotion you were in line for, but when the time came they went outside the organization or institution.

Maybe it was for that magic spark that would make your marriage exciting.

Maybe it was for that certain something that would unify and solidify your family.

Maybe it was for that special revelation from God that would answer all your questions.

The bus was supposed to come every fifteen minutes. That event was just down the road . . . right around the corner . . . almost here. But a quarter of an hour became a half hour . . . then three quarters . . . then an hour . . . then . . . And perhaps you wait still.

For too many people, life has been spent waiting for that something else. And they woke up one day to discover that life had passed them by while they waited for something else.

Life is for living. Life is to be lived in the present, the right now. It is too precious to spend just waiting. And the most productive wait where the time passes the quickest is always that spent in something worthwhile. This is something of what Paul had in mind when he said to the Christians in Rome, "And that, knowing the time, that now it is high time to awake out of sleep: for now is salvation nearer than when we believed" (Rom. 13:11).

The bus comes every fifteen minutes. How are you spending those minutes?

JAMES E. CARTER

Romans 13:11-12 The Lost

The world's population can be divided into approximately three groups. Of the over four billion people on the face of the earth today, we can place at least one-fourth of this population (over a billion people) in a category of those who name Jesus as Lord. About a fourth of the world's population consists of people who do not name him as Lord but who have at least heard of him—at least know his name. Then about one-half of the world's population (over two billion people) have never even heard the name of Jesus. (These figures come from the Lausane Committee on World Evangelism, 1978.)

J. DIXON FREE

Romans 13:11-13 Opportunity

One evening just about sundown while fishing for bass, I threw out a nice chugging plug. I chugged it a time or two then started to reel in when the whole bottom of the lake exploded under it. I had without doubt the biggest fish I had ever had on the end of my line.

I tried to do everything just right. And he did everything bass know how to do.

Finally, I got him up to the side of the boat. He was a big beauty. Since I didn't have a landing net, I asked my fishing partner to reach over and catch him by the gills to lift him in the boat. He plunged his hand over the side of the boat to grab him. And when that happened the fish made one last desperate lunge, broke the line, and got away. The next day I bought me a landing net.

Aren't all of us guilty of making provision for something after it is too late? We get concerned about a person's spiritual condition after he is gone. We worry about our children's companions after they get in trouble. We wonder whether an action was proper after we do it. We get worked up over an issue after it is decided.

There is a proverb for it. It is called shutting the barn door after the horse has gotten out.

There is also a Scripture for it. The apostle Paul wrote: "Besides this you know what hour it is, how it is full time now for you to wake from sleep. For salvation is nearer to us now than when we first believed; the night is far gone, the day is at hand. Let us then cast off the works of darkness and put on the armor of light; let us conduct ourselves becomingly as in the day" (Rom. 13:11-13, RSV).

Why not reverse it though? Why not plan ahead some and try to determine how you can prepare yourself for the problems, possibilities, and events of life?

James E. Carter

Romans 13:11-14 Service

My wife and I lived in San Antonio, Texas, when we were newlyweds. We ate frequently at a restaurant named Earl Abel's. There were a lot of signs with catchy messages on them in one of the dining rooms. Those signs announced such things as: "Eating at home keeps you able; eating here keeps Earl Abel;" and "It was a brave man who ate the first oyster." The sign by the big wall clock over the door read, "This clock will never be stolen; the employees are always watching it."

Paul called on saints to be mindful of the time but for a different reason. He was aware that we don't have an unlimited amount of time to do the work God has assigned. The Christian must serve with his eye on the clock of life, mindful that one day God will announce, "It's quitting time."

Hardy Denham

Romans 14:1-15 The Spirit that Does not Judge

Ester Harding has said that the mystery of the human heart is closed when we judge one another. We really never get to know the person. I came to understand this point one evening when our church had a Quaker Communion service. There was a time of silence then members were encouraged to stand and speak as the Spirit moved them. I will never forget the first man who came forward to speak that night. He began by saying: "I want to thank this church for standing by me. I want to thank my wife for all she has put up with during these last few terrible months. I will never forget my debt to her—or to you."

Everyone present in that room knew his story. He was a deacon, and he had been caught with another man's wife. The community gossip traveled fast, and before long everyone knew the sordid details. But the church refused to judge its member. Here and there some members, of course, did. But as a whole, the church refused to judge this man who had failed so miserably.

They accepted him as he was. Through the weeks and months that followed, he began to find his way to a faith he had never known before. In learning acceptance and forgiveness from the fellowship, he came to know the acceptance and forgiveness of God firsthand. If they had clobbered him or ignored him or even judged him, I wonder what would have happened to that broken man? Instead, they recognized in him some of their own failings and weaknesses and sins that had never surfaced. In that understanding, by refusing to use their critical powers, the man found his way back to service, to faith, and to his family.

ROGER LOVETTE

Romans 14:4 Judging Others

Byron J. Langenfeld said: "Rare is the person who can weigh the faults of others without putting his thumb on the scales."

Robert Burns wrote: "What's done we partly can compute, but know not what's resisted."

HARDY DENHAM

Romans 14:7 Interrelatedness

They had a revolution in the West African nation of Liberia. Dr. William R. Tolbert, the president, was assassinated; his wife was imprisoned, and his son was beheaded.

Normally, we would read the newspaper account of the revolution, shake our heads, and say, "That's too bad, isn't it?" We don't feel much personal impact from an event that occurred half a world away.

But we were not unaffected by this event. Even though it was a long way off and was far removed from us geographically, it is not far removed from us. Let me show some ways in which we are directly related to those events.

Take, first, the late president of the nation. Dr. William R. Tolbert was also a Baptist minister. He served as president of the Baptist World Alliance from 1965-1970. Through the Baptist brotherhood, we have very close ties with what happened there.

I have a friend who is a Southern Baptist missionary in Liberia. We were college classmates. All of the Southern Baptist missionaries and their families were safe. Through shared experiences, we have very close ties with what happened there.

We have a member of our church, a student at Texas Christian University, who is a native of Liberia. For a while following the revolution, she was not able to hear from her family. What happens to the family of any of our church family affects us. Through Christian fellowship, we have very close ties with what happened there.

Marshall McLuhan has called the world a "global village." When we reflect upon both how quickly we become aware of what happens at other places and how we are directly impacted by such far-off occurrences, we can understand the terminology.

John Donne so many years ago said, "No man is an island, entire of itself" (Devotions, No. 17). And these events help us to realize how closely interrelated we truly are.

Paul the apostle reminded us, "For none of us liveth to himself, and no man dieth to himself" (Rom. 14:7).

Life is interrelated. We are impacted by events that seem remote. Therefore, we cannot be flippant, unconcerned, or uncaring about what goes on in the world. We are personally and directly affected by it in strange and unusual ways. It becomes all the more important, then, for Christians to make the world a better place to live both by personal work and effort—and by Christian missions.

JAMES E. CARTER

Romans 14:7-8 For Christ's Sake

Paul reminded us that, whether we are living or dying, the Lord is with us. Johann Sebastian Bach was one of the greatest composers of religious music the world has ever known. Bach was a devout Christian and wrote at the top of every piece of music he ever began: *Jesu, Juva* (Jesus, aid!) After he had labored and written the score of the music he would always scrawl the same words: *soli Deo gloria* (to God alone be glory). Not a bad way to begin a sermon or a life or a marriage or any job. There are the beginnings where the lines are muddled, and we do not know which way to go: Jesus help. And, at the end, when all is finished and we have done all that we can do: to God alone be the glory. "If we live, we live to the Lord, and if we die, we die to the Lord" (v. 8, RSV).

ROGER LOVETTE

Romans 14:7-9 Facing Death

Everyman is a medieval morality play about how each human must one day meet death. Death comes to call Everyman. The victim pleads that he be allowed to seek someone who will go with him on the final fearful journey. He is allowed time to find a traveling companion. One after the other he calls on friends and acquaintances for support. Kinsman, Worldly Goods, Strength, and even Good Deeds are all contacted. Each has an excuse or reason why he cannot accompany Everyman on his terrible, final journey. It is a parable with a lesson for each human being. In the final analysis, only Faith could lend support. So it is for every person in every age. Only Christ, through faith, can offer strength to overcome the last great enemy.

RAYMOND H. BAILEY

Romans 14:10-12 Judging Others

Harsh judgments of others can develop over a long period of time or can be made in the emotions of the moment; either way the damage may be severe. In a committee meeting, animated by the nature of a particular issue, one man made a one-sentence statement. Another man quickly retorted, "That's the stupidest statement I ever heard in my life!" There was a long silence. Several members tried to move the meeting along, but the damage had been done, and the meeting adjourned without any sign of progress.

Paul implied that our judgments upon others may be more carefully and seldom given if we considered first that each of us will ourselves be judged by God.

Abraham Lincoln spoke to us all in the familiar quotation, "There is so much good in the worst of us and so much bad in the best of us, that it does not behoove any of us to talk about the rest of us."

I enjoyed an evening at dinner with several ministers. An out-of-town minister, in whose honor the dinner was given, offered a timely observation about judging others: "We overestimate the strengths of others; we underestimate their needs."

W. Wayne Price

Romans 14:13-23 A Stumbling Block

In the last century, Henry Ward Beecher rose to be one of the most famous ministers of his age. While pastor of the Plymouth Church in Brooklyn, New York, Beecher went on trial for adulterous behavior with Elizabeth Tilton. The trial lasted six months and received more space in the newspaper than any event since the Civil War. Although he was found innocent of the charge, many, including the historian Milton Rugoff, and newspapers like *The New York Times* and the Louisville *Courier-Journal*, believed he was guilty of the charge and escaped only because of great wealth and powerful lawyers.

Whether he was guilty of the charge of adultery is not easy to determine today, but he was certainly guilty of serious acts of indiscretion and poor judgment. This scandal hurt the cause of Christ and caused many to question the distance between what one said and the way he lived. The stronger Christian needs to guard his life against temptation, lest his fall damage not only himself but others who look to him for an example of moral living and leadership.

William P. Tuck

Romans 14:14 Responsibility

According to a Greek legend, Prometheus had the responsibility to oversee creation and give to man and the animals the faculties necessary for preservation. Prometheus began to bestow gifts on the animals. When time came to bestow a gift on man, Prometheus discovered that he had exhausted his gifts. He had been ordered to bestow upon man a special gift, but he had nothing to give. At the advice of Athene, the goddess of wisdom, Prometheus lighted a torch at the chariot of the sun god and brought to earth fire as the supreme gift to man. Man would use fire to cook his food, heat his dwelling, and fashion tools and weapons with which to subdue the other animals.

Zeus, the king of all the gods, became angry when he discovered man had the gift of fire, for he believed that fire was to be reserved only to the gods. Zeus, therefore, proclaimed that man must pay for his intrusion upon the properties of the gods. Prometheus had brought fire to man as a blessing; Zeus ordered that it should become a curse as well. For every hearth that it warmed, it would burn another house to the ground. For every forge used to make weapons, another would explode in conflagration to destroy man. For every field tilled with tools forged from fire, another would be ravaged by fire. Thus Prometheus' gift became a mixed blessing for man. Whether fire was a gift from Prometheus or a curse from Zeus would be determined by man.

What the Greek legend affirms about fire, Paul concluded about every aspect of life. "I know and am convinced in the Lord Jesus that nothing is unclean in itself; but to him who thinks anything to be unclean, to him it is unclean" (NASB). Will life be a curse or a blessing to us? It depends on what we make of it.

BRIAN L. HARBOUR

Romans 14:16 Doing Good

At nineteen years of age, I became pastor of the First Baptist Church of Pearson, Oklahoma. I was a college sophomore, single, inexperienced, and knew nothing about growing a congregation. I decided to visit every family in that small community and invite them to attend our church. A teenaged girl opened the door of the first house I visited. She invited me in. I asked after sitting down if her mother were home. She replied that she was the woman of the house. I visited a few minutes, invited her to our services, and left. The following week several church members reported to me that this girl had gone all over the community bragging about the young preacher visiting her when her husband wasn't at home. I learned my lesson well, early in my ministry, even doing good can "be evil spoken of."

BILL BRUSTER

Romans 14:19 Peace

Mitsuo Fuchida led the Japanese air attack on Pearl Harbor, the action which plunged the United States into World War II.

Fuchida developed a bitter hatred for Americans because he heard a report that Americans tortured Japanese prisoners. His hatred grew with the atomic bombing of Hiroshima and Nagasaki.

After the war he sought evidence of American atrocities against the Japanese in order that he might publicize them. Instead he found many instances of kind treatment. One of his friends told him how the daughter of missionaries who had been killed by Japanese soldiers in the Philippines had taken care of captive Japanese soldiers and nursed them back to health with love and gentleness.

This impressed him. Soon after that, he received a tract that told about the conversion of an American bombardier in a Japanese prison. A Japanese guard had given the American a Bible, and the American had been converted. The American had hated the Japanese, but then his hate had changed to love.

Fuchida secured a Bible. The prayer of Jesus in Luke 23:34 became his example. Fuchida said, "I met Jesus that day. He came into my heart and changed my life from a military officer to a warrior for Christ." He refused an appointment to a high position in the Japanese Air Force and began to preach the gospel of Christ. He became one of Japan's greatest evangelists and has even preached in the United States.[26]

ELMER L. GRAY

Romans 15:1 Burden Bearing

William Muehl, seminary professor and astute observer of human nature, relates a story which rings a bell for all parents. He remembers waiting in the lobby of a nursery school for the children about to begin Christmas recess. They came pouring out of the classroom, carrying the gifts they had been preparing for weeks. One little boy came forth putting on his coat, waving and running all at the same time, slipped and fell. His carefully prepared gift for his mom and dad went crashing to the floor with him. When he realized that his gift was broken, he burst forth into a torrent of sobs. His father, trying his best to comfort him, knelt down and said, "Now, it doesn't matter, Son. It really doesn't matter." But his mother, much more in tune with the boy's emotions and needs, bent down and drew the little fellow into her arms and said, "Oh but it does matter. It matters a great deal." And she wept with him.[27]

They who are strong ought to bear the burdens of the weak. And they can, if they remember what it means to be weak.

W. Wayne Price

Romans 15:1-6 Bearing the Weak

George Thomas tells of Bill and Betty Price of Boston, Massachusetts, who were told in 1949 that their seven-year-old son Billy had a severe case of muscular dystrophy and would not live past the age of fourteen. The mother would not accept the prognosis and devoted her life to making Billy want to live.

It is a marvelous story of how one person's love kept another alive. With Billy's muscles severely contracted so that he had to be strapped in his wheelchair, his mother helped him prepare for and pass the Scholastic Aptitude Test. She also taught him to play chess.

In 1968, when Billy was twenty-six years old, his mother died of cancer. She died on Sunday. Billy viewed her body on Tuesday. The funeral was on Wednesday. Thursday, with no discernible medical change, Billy died.

David Matthews

Romans 15:1-8 Brotherhood

The Russian historian Tolstoy told of a Russian beggar seeking money during a famine. Tolstoy wanted to help but had no money. He took the beggar's hand and said, "Don't be angry with me, Brother. I have nothing to give." The beggar's face brightened, "But you *have* given me something; you called me brother, and that is a greater gift than money." To love others as brothers is to give ourselves, and the supreme example is Christ.

Bill D. Whittaker

Romans 15:5-6 Cooperation

A man was standing behind a large crate which seemed to be stuck in a door through which he was trying to move the crate. A fellow worker, seeing his dilemma, offered to help. He went around through another door to the other side of the crate. After several moments of huffing and puffing, the newcomer said, "I don't think we are ever going to get this crate in the room."

"In?" replied the other worker. "I'm not trying to get it in. I'm trying to get it out."

What a picture of the church! Christians often put out effort but accomplish nothing because they are working against each other. How we need to live by the admonition of Paul to the Romans: "Now may the God who gives perseverance and encouragement grant you to be of the same mind with one another according to Christ Jesus; that with one accord you may with one voice glorify the God and Father of our Lord Jesus Christ" (NASB).

BRIAN L. HARBOUR

Romans 15:9 Sing and Rejoice

Hope, glorify, rejoice, sing are some of the words Paul used in the fifteenth chapter to provide Christians assurance in God's love. The phrase "and sing unto thy name" denotes the music of the soul that moves us to deep emotions.

Music has always expressed these stirring feelings of our heart. Irving Berlin, one of America's greatest songwriters, had the gift of doing this. In 1918, while stationed in the army on Long Island, he wrote "God Bless America" for a camp show. For some reason he didn't think it was appropriate for the times. It wasn't published until 1938 when threats of World War II became apparent. During the following war years, "God

Bless America" became a veritable national anthem. The song took on additional significance when it was recalled that Irving Berlin was born in Russia. His appreciation of his adopted country was, indeed, a deep commitment of joy that made the music of the soul cry out for expression.

We, as Christians, have a song to sing that never grows old. It is the soul's hymn of hope that springs from the music in our hearts.

JACK GULLEDGE

Romans 15:13 Joy

I was visiting with a friend recently who is a long-time employee of a state institution in another state. He was talking about the time he had put in with that institution, their retirement policies, and when he would be eligible for retirement. He indicated that he is strongly considering taking retirement as soon as he is eligible and then going into another line of work. Then he said, "It just isn't as much fun around here as it used to be." Life had taken on a grimness.

If you don't think that is a true statement, take a seat in a mall and study the faces of the people you see pass by. Tune your ears to the remarks in the grocery store checkout line. Listen to the comments as people discuss government, education, economy, or denominational life.

Grimness takes its toll. Elton Trueblood was right when he wrote not too long ago, "Though there are today some happy people, we do not live in a happy age. Millions admit that they have lost hope and feel trapped. Since they see no way out for themselves or for the nation, they can envision no solution to their problems—financial, occupational, or matrimonial."

This kind of grimness in life issues in hopeless, meaningless, and discouraged living. Many people go to work each day with no sense of accomplishment and joy only a sense of duty and necessity. Stephen Vincent Benet wrote:

> Life is not lost by dying! Life is lost
> Minute by minute, day by dragging day,
> In all the thousand, small, uncaring ways.

What is the Christian to do in this kind of grim atmosphere? First, know that we are to live for Christ in whatever kind of time we are called to live. Second, we can refuse to take ourselves too seriously. Third, remember that faith in Christ brings hope and joy. Paul wrote to some Christians at Rome in another grim time. To them he said, "May the God of hope fill you with all joy and peace in believing, so that by the power of the Holy Spirit you may abound in hope" (Rom. 15:13, RSV). Fourth, live with the "holy hilarity" Christ introduces into life.

When life get grim turn again to the Christ who gives hope and hilarity to allow us to face even grim times in purpose and peace.

JAMES E. CARTER

Romans 15:17-21 Only Christ

In the early 1960s, the heroic Christian leader Martin Niemöller came to America on a speaking tour. Knowing of his experience under the Hitler regime and of his resistance to the Nazis, two newspaper reporters hurried to hear him, expecting a sensational discussion of those war years.

After listening to Dr. Niemöller preach a genuine gospel message, they left the church disappointed. One reporter said to the other, "Six years in a Nazi prison camp, and all he has to talk about is Jesus Christ."

DAVID MATTHEWS

Romans 15:22 When Things Don't Go Your Way

Paul had a burning desire to go to Rome, and he shared that desire with the Roman saints (see Rom. 1:9-12). However, in spite of that desire, he had been unable to go to Rome (see Rom. 1:13). It was a situation of things not going as he wanted them to.

Yet, there are times in life when things don't go your way. Someone wrote an article on the theme, "You know it's going to be a bad day when:"

Here are a few of the indications. You know it's going to be a bad day when you wake up face down on the pavement; when you call Suicide Prevention and they put you on hold; when you see the "Sixty Minutes" news team in your office; when your twin sister forgets your birthday; when your horn accidentally starts blowing and you are following a group of Hell's Angels.

Life must have contingency plans for the days when things don't go your way.

HARDY DENHAM

Romans 15:24 Disappointment

Paul hoped to visit Rome enroute to mission work in Spain. History indicates that his desire was frustrated. He got to Rome but was tried and executed.

There are times when our plans go awry, and our efforts end in failure. Still, God can bring good out of evil (Rom. 8:28). John Wesley was an Anglican missionary to the colony of Georgia—but he was unsuccessful as a missionary. He returned to England. Wesley was later able to send George Whitfield to preach in colonial America. Whitfield had a remarkable ministry for thirty years. He preached from Georgia to New England with great effectiveness. He led in the first Great Awakening in this country. Meanwhile back in England, Wesley's preaching brought revival to England and the founding of Methodism.

ALTON H. MCEACHERN

Romans 15:26-27 Giving: Opportunity and Obligation

A widow with three children once approached her pastor concerning a giving dilemma. Members of her larger family felt she was giving too much to the church. She wanted to be fair and do the right thing, but she felt justified in her generosity. She explained that there had been a time when she could have given much more but didn't. She loved the Lord too much now to give less.

How much a Christian gives is a personal decision. Most Christians, however, feel a sense of oughtness mingled with their free choice. Perhaps it is always as Paul explained about the Gentiles' financial support of the needy Jews. Giving is an opportunity and an obligation.

ERNEST D. STANDERFER

Romans 15:30-33 Prayer

When we told our six-year-old about our plans to go as missionaries to the Philippines she asked, "Is it so far away that when I call Courtney [her best friend and next-door neighbor] it will be long distance?" Every missionary joins with Paul in an appeal to the churches "to strive together with me in your prayers to God on my behalf, . . . that my service . . . may be acceptable . . . so that by God's will I may come to you with joy" (vv. 30-32, RSV). Through prayer the distant miles are instantly bridged and co-laborers meet in the Spirit at the throne of grace.

BILL D. WHITTAKER

Romans 16:1-16 Ordinary Christians

Who led you to Christ? For most of us, they were the ordinary people of our lives—our parents, ministers, Sunday School teachers, deacons, friends. Most of the work of Christ is carried on by the ordinary Christians living out their lives in routine ways. Charles Spurgeon, who became one of the most noted preachers of the last century, was converted under the preaching of a lay preacher. Spurgeon turned into a little Primitive Methodist Church on a side street in London when a heavy snowstorm hit.

Only about a dozen or fifteen people were present. Even the regular preacher could not make it. A thin-looking man, who was a tailor or shoemaker, was preaching. His text was "Look unto me, and be ye saved, all ye ends of the earth" (Isa. 45:22). Spurgeon said the man could not even pronounce the words correctly, but he noted that the text called upon persons to look unto Jesus. Finally the lay preacher turned to Spurgeon and fixed his eyes upon him and declared: "Young man, you look very miserable. And you always will be miserable—miserable in life, miserable in death—if you don't obey my text; but if you obey now, this moment, you will be saved." The preacher then lifted his hand and shouted: "Young man, look to Jesus Christ. Look! Look! Look! You have nothing to do but to look and live." Spurgeon said that he saw at once the way of salvation, and the cloud of darkness rolled away from his life, and he saw the sun. An ordinary Christian layman had led this young man to Christ.[28]

Romans 16 is filled with the names of early Christian leaders who were the ordinary people God used in the first century to share his good news. Most of them are only names to us, but they were God's servants, like we are today, spreading the good news of Christ with others.

WILLIAM P. TUCK

Romans 16:1-16 Women

Li-Ti-Ou was one of the "weaker sex." She stood less than 4′3″ tall and, during the illness that eventually resulted in death, weighed less than a hundred pounds. She did not live out the role assigned to the women of her culture. She never married, and she did men's work, probably the work of ten strong men. Li-Ti-Ou was the Chinese name of Charlotte Digges Moon, better known as Lottie Moon and universally recognized as a foremost example of Southern Baptist foreign missions. To this day her example provides the conscience and inspiration for SBC foreign mission work. She preached the gospel across China to men and women who would have died without hearing it if they had had to wait for a man to proclaim it. Surely we join her plea "that other women and many of them be sent."

She was undoubtedly a woman like Phoebe and the others who Paul said should be received as "befits the saints" (v. 2, RSV).

RAYMOND H. BAILEY

Romans 16:1-27 Thanksgiving

As Paul came to the close of his letter, his mind was filled with thanksgiving for those persons who had shared his life.

Not long ago I received a letter from a father who wrote to say thank you for helping his son through a difficult time in his life. A few years ago two former students who had been critical of my teaching came up to me at the Louisiana Baptist Convention and said, "You'll never know how much you mean to us."

The longer I live the more I have come to realize that the things that give life meaning and purpose are not those things that can be locked away in a safe-deposit box or added up in a bank statement. They are relationships, experiences with God in Christ in our service to others. The things that make the heart beat a bit faster and make life worth living are the smile of my wife and a hand squeezed across the table, my daughter who thanks me with a hug for making life meaningful for her, my son smiling and saying that he appreciated all my effort, or the student who expresses appreciation for the teaching he received.

Paul set a wonderful example for us. He never ceased to thank God for life's relationships.

JAMES A. YOUNG

Romans 16:12-15 The Faithful

On the occasion of his ninety-fourth birthday celebration, statesman Bernard Baruch was asked to name the greatest person of his generation. He replied, "The fellow who does his job every day."

Many persons, relatively unknown for their heroic faithfulness to the cause of Christ, make up the ranks of those who do their job day after day. Paul recognized that God uses faithful persons to extend his kingdom and to enable others to record outstanding achievements in Christian service.

ERNEST D. STANDERFER

Romans 16:13 Rufus's Mother

In the last chapter of the Book of Romans Paul became practical. He began to name some of the people that had been special to him. And in the middle of all those names we bump into a strange verse: 'Greet Rufus, . . . also his mother and mine." Now we know that Rufus was not Paul's real, blood brother. Rufus's mother was not, in reality, Paul's real mother. Why did he say that Rufus's mother was his mother too? Old, grey hair in a bun, in her seventies, with an apron on, she had taken Paul in. She had served him sumptuous meals. Far from home, she had loved him and affirmed him and made him feel special. So Paul felt for Rufus's mother the affection that her own son felt. The gospel often comes to us like that.

ROGER LOVETTE

Notes

1. James E. Carter, "It's Dynamite!" in *Award Winning Sermons,* vol. II (Nashville: Broadman Press, 1978), pp. 11-12.
2. Quoted in Roland H. Bainton, *Here I Stand* (New York: New American Library, 1950), pp. 49-50.
3. Karl Menninger, *Whatever Became of Sin?* (New York: E. P. Dutton, 1973).
4. Lynn H. Hough, *The Dignity of Man* (Nashville: Abingdon, 1950), p. 75.
5. William Faulkner, copyright 1963 by Postscript.
6. Gordon W. Allport quoted by James Poling in *Glamour,* Feb. 1957. © The Condé Nast Publication, Inc., NY, NY.
7. James E. Carter, *Christ and the Crowds* (Nashville: Broadman Press, 1981), p. 7.
8. Shakespeare, *Macbeth,* Act V, Sc. iii.

9. James E. Carter, "Whatever Became of Sin?" in *Salvation in Our Time,* Lavonn D. Brown, ed. (Nashville: Broadman Press, 1978), pp. 45-46.

10. William Barclay, Daily Study Bible, *Luke,* p. 10.

11. Dimitri Drobatschewsky, "'Cheap' violin instrumental in owner's sudden wealth," *The Arizona Republic,* Sept. 16, 1982.

12. Walther B. Knight, *Knight's Masterbook of New Illustrations* (Grand Rapids: Wm. B. Eerdman's Publishing Co., 1958), p. 351.

13. John Milton, *Paradise Lost,* Book I, lines 254-263.

14. Daniel Yankelovich, "New Rules in American Life: Searching for Self-Fulfillment in a World Turned Upside Down," *Psychology Today,* April 1981, p. 80.

15. Albert Camus, *The Plague* (New York: Vintage Books, 1972), p. 278.

16. Edgar N. Jackson, *Understanding Prayer* (New York: World Publishing Company, 1968), p. 5.

17. Shakespeare, *Antony and Cleopatra,* Act II, Sc. i.

18. Alexander Maclaren, *Expostions of Holy Scripture* (Grand Rapids: Wm. B. Eerdman's Publishing Co., 1944), p. 199.

19. L. D. Johnson, *The Morning After Death* (Nashville: Broadman Press, 1978), p. 113.

20. Based on "The Bible in America," *Newsweek,* Dec. 27, 1982, p. 44.

21. *The Commission,* Jan. 1983, p. 5.

22. Adapted from "Getting the Most Out of Life," The *Reader's Digest* Association, Inc., 1946, p. 18.

23. John Bishop, *Seeing Jesus Today: A Portrait of Jesus the Man* (Valley Forge: Judson Press, 1969), p. 79.

24. Luther Joe Thompson, *Love Is Alive* (Nashville: Broadman Press, 1980), p. 96.

25. Edward Gibbon, *Decline and Fall of the Roman Empire, The Fifty Third Chapter,* Britannica Great Books, Vol 43, p. 327.

26. *The Baptist Program,* Feb. 1981, p. 11.

27. William Muehl, *All the Damned Angels* (Philadelphia: Pilgrim Press, 1972), p. 29.

28. *C. H. Spurgeon's Autobiography,* ed. and condensed by David O. Fuller (Grand Rapids: Zondervan Publishing House, 1946), pp. 39-41.

Index